AF413838

BANNING BOOKS
IN AMERICA

BANNING BOOKS IN AMERICA

Not a How-to

EDITED BY SAMUEL COHEN

BLOOMSBURY ACADEMIC

NEW YORK • LONDON • OXFORD • NEW DELHI • SYDNEY

BLOOMSBURY ACADEMIC
Bloomsbury Publishing Inc, 1359 Broadway, New York, NY 10018, USA
Bloomsbury Publishing Plc, 50 Bedford Square, London, WC1B 3DP, UK
Bloomsbury Publishing Ireland, 29 Earlsfort Terrace, Dublin 2, D02 AY28, Ireland

BLOOMSBURY, BLOOMSBURY ACADEMIC and the Diana logo are
trademarks of Bloomsbury Publishing Plc

First published in the United States of America 2026

Cover design: Eleanor Rose
Cover image © Getty image; Additional image © Alamy

Library of Congress Cataloging-in-Publication Data
Names: Cohen, Samuel S. editor
Title: Banning books in America : not a how-to / edited by Samuel Cohen.
Description: New York : Bloomsbury Academic, 2026. |
Includes bibliographical references and index.
Identifiers: LCCN 2025033571 | ISBN 9798765138076 hardback |
ISBN 9798765138069 paperback | ISBN 9798765138083 pdf |
ISBN 9798765138090 epub
Subjects: LCSH: Censorship–United States | Challenged books–United States |
Prohibited books–United States | Intellectual freedom–United States |
LCGFT: Essays
Classification: LCC Z658.U5 B37 2026
LC record available at https://lccn.loc.gov/2025033571

ISBN: HB: 979-8-7651-3807-6
          ePDF: 979-8-7651-3808-3
          eBook: 979-8-7651-3809-0

Typeset by Integra Software Services Private Limited.
Printed and bound in the United States of America

For product safety related questions contact productsafety@bloomsbury.com.

To find out more about our authors and books visit www.bloomsbury.com
and sign up for our newsletters.

To the book protectors

CONTENTS

PART THREE Teachers on Book Banning 103

Introduction

Samuel Cohen

This is a book about book banning in America, and so it is a book about America.

The administration occupying the White House during the time of this book's publication has spent its first months in office attacking the foundations of our society, unlawfully withdrawing funding from and restricting the work of agencies and institutions that work to keep people fed, healthy, educated, and protected from discrimination. Members and state officials of this administration's party have spent the past few years attacking these same agencies and institutions, from the Department of Education to their local public libraries and schools. These attacks include attempts to control access to books.

Like many of us, I have watched in horror and anger over the last few years as the country has returned to the culture wars of the 1990s, which were themselves a return to the Red Scare 1950s, which were in turn a return to all of the times in our history that some of those in power have benefitted and even encouraged division and demonization. I come from the Northeast, but I have lived in the southern Midwest for twenty-some years now and so have had a front-row seat for the use of rhetorical political violence, the kind that can lead to physical violence. The entire nation is now seeing the violence a society can do to its most vulnerable members—people whose sexuality, gender, race, and economic condition make them vulnerable in a society riddled with bigotry and selfishness—and to anyone who wants to live in a just society.

The scenes of mass firings, of deportation, of American soldiers deployed on American streets are terrifying and enraging, but should be no more so than the scenes from school board meetings and legislative sessions in which citizens and lawmakers attempt to strip the rights to free expression and inquiry from those who need them most. The scenes of concerned citizens trying to remove access to books by and about these most vulnerable people are often the result of astroturfing—that is, they appear to but don't actually arise from grassroots movements, instead being constructed by national advocacy organizations telling these citizens what books to challenge, without of course requiring they be read first. There's a violence to that too, to the books themselves, unread, to their authors, unheard, and to potential readers, pawns in larger political games. Rubber bullets and book bans are weapons deployed against all of us. This is a dangerous moment. Our rights to due process, to fair treatment, to representative democracy, to the freedom to read and write what we want, are at stake.

✱✱✱

This is a book about book banning. Before you object that there are no real book bans, at least not anymore, at least not in the US: okay, fine. Then this is a book about attempts by people to keep other people from reading books by curtailing their access to them in one way or another. Admittedly, these ways generally fall short of outright government bans of the books' very existence: they include removing them from classrooms, from school library shelves, from public library shelves, but laws banning their existence are rare and, historically in the US, are overturned in court. Nonetheless, with objections and qualifications noted, people have been very busy in the last five or so years trying to take books out of classrooms, off of shelves, and out of backpacks and back pockets.

So what this book is really about is access to books: about the efforts taken to restrict access; about the motivations of the people trying to restrict access, professed and actual; about the books to which they are trying to restrict access; about efforts to restore access and the motivations of those making those efforts; about the larger cultural contexts in which people would fight over books. A book about these things needs to spend some time examining the American context in which these things happen, historically and right now, so this book is also a book about the country. A book about these things also has to spend some time considering what books mean to people, what they use them for and love them for and fear them for and hate them for. What books do, then, and what people think they can do, ought to do, even ought not to do—these are also topics that need to be considered.

I have put this book together because I'm angry, even though, as many people and some who have written pieces in it argue, there's not much in the way of actual banning happening. It's the attempts as much as the outcomes. I've also put this book together because of all the questions the attempts raise. These are the same reasons I teach my course on banned books. The course is a way for me to assign books that some Americans have decided other Americans shouldn't get to read. It's a way for me to help my students think about why these particular books have been challenged and what would be lost if people didn't get to read them. And it's a way for us to think about the larger issues of censorship, freedom, identity, and discrimination that animate these arguments. I've tried to give a sense of these discussions in my contribution to the book, the closing "A Banned Books Course Syllabus with Historical Notes, Unfortunate Puns, and Books, Lots of Books." As the overstuffed title indicates, it's a sometimes comically expanded version of my actual course syllabus that tries to point in the direction of the many rabbit holes we go down in the course when we investigate the subject of banned books in the US; it also tries to express the wonder and joy of reading these books that people are trying to keep from us. My hope for you, its reader, is that its covert and not-so-covert points, brief digressions, and not always entirely necessary footnotes amount to a useful argument for reading and teaching these books and for thinking about why we should be free to do so. My hope for myself, one I express only sheepishly, is that it honors my pre-teen self, raiding my parents' shelves of paperbacks and my school library for Asimov and Vonnegut and Updike, confused but excited by what they showed me about my world and by the new different worlds they imagined, and that it goes some measure toward the protection of that kid's right to read those books or any other books he found on any shelves anywhere.

Thanks to the curiosity, generosity, and conviction of the authors of the following chapters, this book offers a variety of lenses through which readers can consider these topics. In Part One, "Writers on Book Banning," we get the point of view of novelists considering the possibility of having access to their works restricted. In Part Two, "Arguments About Book Banning," we hear from a wide range of activists, administrators, and academics who present a diverse set of arguments about the challenging, censoring, and banning of books. Part Three, "Teachers on Book Banning," offers a set of reflections on educational access to literature in national and international contexts and in the contexts of university and secondary education.

It is my hope that you will read everything in this collection. Reading these chapters will, I hope, encourage you to engage with a wider range of ideas about the current moment's frenzy of hostility to books, to examine your assumptions about access, education, and government's role in both, and to commit yourself, should you find the problem worthy of your efforts, to addressing it in the world in which you live, vote, and read. The joke of the book's subtitle, *Not a How-to*, is that this is not a guide to banning books, a *Book Banning for Idiots*. The hope hidden in the joke is that it will be a *How Not-to*, an inspiration for thinking further and even fighting back against the organizations and forces that would tell us what we can and cannot read. In a country where people in power seem intensely interested in controlling the free flow of information and ideas, we need other people to be devoted to making sure that the books through which flows so much of what we think and know are available to all.

PART ONE

WRITERS ON BOOK BANNING

1

The Woodcutters

Lydia Millet

When a friend wrote to me some months ago that he'd heard a book of mine had been banned, I felt a surge of excitement. I'm not proud of this.

The banning of a book is hardly a badge of literary merit, after all: plenty of otherwise unmemorable books have been the targets of pushes to ban, along with excellent and important books, as have a variety of fairly unremarkable artistic outputs in other media that have captured the attention of censorship movements.

Clearly this is because it's mainly content, rather than form or style, that raises red flags for those drawn to the act of suppressing artistic expression (though attitude, as an aspect or modulation of style, may serve to notify the wary of potentially naughty content). In contemporary US politics a fear of the creeping normalization of otherness appears to be inspiring banning initiatives, apparently rooted in the premise that sympathetic portrayals of that otherness, as embodied in the voices of marginalized individuals or groups, are seductive and therefore dangerous.

Still, the will to ban a text is a signal of impact: it indicates that a creative product presents a perceived insult either to power structures or to the self-appointed guardians of an ideology or status quo. In other words, the gesture of banning suggests social relevance. Hooray!

As it turned out, my friend was mistaken. None of my books had ever been banned, sadly.

For *years* I've been writing fiction with disreputable content! I thought indignantly. Nay, decades! Novel after novel in which the unsavory characteristics of various invented people, chiefly my fellow Americans, are explored at exuberant length! I devoted an entire book to the hapless exploits of a misogynist pornographer with messianic delusions (*Everyone's Pretty*). Another one featured child trafficking, rape, and torture (*My Happy Life*). More recently, there was a graphic short story in which a drug-addled pedophile has sex with his underage stepdaughter (*Fight No More*).

And in return for all that scurrilous effort, not a single banning. Not even a modest local-library-shelf kerfuffle. Not a peep.

In my disappointment, mulling over the rewards and punishments of my chosen field, I recalled passages in *Woodcutters*, a novel by Austrian writer Thomas Bernhard (which itself was a bestseller before it was ordered pulped after a defamation lawsuit).

Woodcutters sets forth the musings of a narrator sitting in an armchair at a dinner party who excoriates the literary awards establishments of his native land (and by extension all lands that are host to a robust bourgeoisie). Over the course of a hilarious interior monologue of relentless judgment, he roundly condemns both the institutions that bestow such awards and the writers who covet and/or smugly accept them as sycophants and hacks, respectively. The result of this dynamic tension of bootlickers, according to Bernhard's narrator, is the perpetual elevation and official anointment of mediocrity.

I've found myself on both sides of the Bernhardian sycophant-hack equation a few times, I guess, serving on the juries of a couple of fancy prizes with my peers and receiving occasional mentions of my own work on one ego-boosting list or another, and it has always seemed to me that Bernhard's fictional speaker was essentially correct.

Now and then a groundbreaking work of art slips through the dragnet of compromise to garner an accolade, but more typically, in the event that an awards committee is faced with a genuinely unique and formally challenging opus as a contender, a sense of vague discomfort settles upon the assembled company. And at that point, ushered into the floating mists of non-consensus with murmurings of political unease regarding content or intellectual befuddlement regarding style, the briefly sighted, singular beast of language vanishes from the visible landscape. Soon to become locally or functionally extinct.

An award is the opposite of a banning, proclaiming: Many smart people in this sovereign nation, perhaps a critical mass, value your contribution. While a banning tries to assert the obverse: that a book should be outlawed because it could harm the collective by glorifying (someone's conception of) moral turpitude—threatening, say, to lure impressionable youth into a sticky web of nonconforming personal identity or sexuality. In the current version of the United States, most of the pressure to ban wishes to style itself as ground-up and community-based, but the funding and mobilization of this "grassroots" can often be traced back to gray eminences of the political right pursuing an exclusionary agenda on civil rights.

Under authoritarian governments, banning comes directly from the top and no grassroots class-washing is called for.

Of course neither an award nor a banning is an accurate barometer of the originality or beauty of a thing, and the marketplace that determines whether a book is read by eager millions or six gentle poets in quiet contemplation is a poor barometer as well.

In free-market terms, both prizegiving and censorship drives qualify as manipulations of the cultural economy—advertising aimed at increasing demand for one brand or exemplar over another, in the case of awards, or in the case of bans, propaganda aimed at decreasing supply by making a piece of language less available to the public. Such intrusions into the circuit of buying and selling are inevitable, needless to say: capitalism without advertising and propaganda would be a paltry system indeed, more akin to a legless, armless and slow-moving creature like a worm than a ferocious and all-consuming tiger. If only.

And generally, in book publishing as in other businesses, budgets are required to advertise; budgets are derived from past revenues; past revenues are derived from past sales; and those past sales have occurred, at least in part, through past advertising, whether paid or unpaid (reviews, book clubs, celebrity endorsements, word of mouth). This means that the successful propagation of a book by a publishing entity usually depends on its successful propagation of previous books.

In theory awards are an alternate vehicle of earned advertising, existing, in their ideal iteration, to recognize fine work that the market has overlooked. In practice they tend to promote middlebrow forms of storytelling that rely on familiar idioms and safe signposts of high-mindedness, but nonetheless: their existence offers a pathway to the celebration of subtle and nuanced language in a society where subtlety and nuance are under siege. And in that role, I'd argue, they do more good than harm.

Which is not to say that Bernhard's protagonist had it wrong but merely that mediocrity, in the realm of literature, is preferable to disregard or annihilation. The elevation of mediocre texts has the advantage of continuing a conversation, at least, while the banning of texts, in its shadow-play projection of crude bigotries onto a public stage, furthers repressive silence. And stills the curiosity, communication, and debate on which any self-aware democracy depends.

Book-banning can also have a boomerang effect, in a democracy, since bad publicity is famously better than no publicity and the creation of any taboo invites its willful and thrilling violation. Hence my delight in the brief delusion of my own banning.

That delight was an artifact of privilege, for sure—the privilege of someone working in a heterogeneous sociopolitical space. In decentralized arenas of language production and consumption, the prospect of rejection and erasure from one quarter can be treated with a degree of playfulness because it doesn't necessarily bring with it total rejection, as it would under, for example, an autocratic régime. In fact, total rejection can only come, in a diverse and competitive forum, from the increasingly consolidated publishing establishment itself when it declines to undertake the publication of a manuscript in the first place. And with the proliferation of small presses and the ascendance of self-publishing as viable, if less expeditious or prestigious strategies for writers, even the indifference of mainstream publishers is not always the final word.

It should be mentioned that several book erasures have occurred in US publishing in recent years when a particular volume was deemed censorship-worthy not by the vigilantly value-defensive right but the vigilantly value-defensive left. I remember cases in which books were either summarily withdrawn from planned publication at the eleventh hour or lustily vilified afterward via media furors that erupted on the subject of their authorship—self-righteous squabbles over whether a given author had the "right" to generate the fictional content in question. Such cancellations are a blot on the escutcheon of the left as certainly as cancellations from the right, and the deference of any publisher to them a mark of rank cowardice.

Propagandistically, cancellations from the left are seldom referred to as bans: bans, one argument may go, happen after publication rather than before or during it. Effectively cancellations *are* bans, however, despite the reluctance of the censorious left to call them by that name (since "banning" is supposed to be the refuge of right-wing scoundrels, right?). They emerge from a similar hysteria of virtue-signaling and result in similar black-listings.

In the wake of leftist cancellations, so-called sensitivity readers have begun to be hired as a mechanism for reassuring a publishing corporation that a piece of writing does not risk the giving of offense to a predetermined set of readers. This paternalistic screening is manifestly also a form of censorship, for censors are censors whether their motivations are noble or base. Censorship is an act, not an intention or feeling.

So is, arguably in softer garb, the trend of trigger warnings, which—mirroring the grim cancer label on a pack of cigarettes—dull the impact of a product or dissuade users entirely by advising them that its consumption may be hazardous to their health. What a trigger warning presumes is that readers are entitled to be protected before the fact from the possibility of powerful emotion, an odd entitlement at best and one that is seldom afforded to any being in the course of the rest of life.

The implication is that art should be a safe space, divested of surprise or shock, into which folk can enter with the polite reassurance that their daily journey through the world will not be substantially disrupted.

This is a direct undermining of the idea of art. The freedom of all speech that is not an incitement to violence or a defamatory or libelous falsehood must be protected as sacred, and the very premise of fiction is that it consists of imagining the lives of others.

Anyone has the "right" to imagine and write anything; anyone has the right to either read it or not read it, enjoy it or not enjoy it, deem it an artistic failure or success; and which categories of others can be imagined by an author should be neither prescribed nor prohibited. The notion that content should align with an author's demographic identity is as chilling and stultifying as any other muzzling. Without the freedom to embark on ambitious experiments in negative capability there would be no *Moby Dicks* or *Anna Kareninas*—no brilliant or meaningful fiction and in the end, really, no fiction. For fiction that fails to challenge preexisting views and assumptions is nothing more than idle chatter—small talk. And small talk may help to pass the time but doesn't invest that time with learning or vibrance or novelty.

The social enterprise of the left is rightly the expansion of enfranchisement and equity, and as I write, that agenda is profoundly embattled, both in the United States and in other countries. Yet the solution is not to shame or pillory those artists who dare to drive outside their assigned lanes. Whatever we call them, and whether they arise from the right or left, campaigns to quash speech are time-wasting, truth-wasting exercises in the denial of social reality.

In the case of literature, though not freeways, adventurous lane-changing should be encouraged. Not only lane-changing, but crossing the median, driving on the shoulder, careering across fields, crashing through barns and outhouses and toolsheds, even slapping wings on the car so that it soars aloft.

At that point the lines painted on the asphalt turn from cages into features of the landscape among many others, and the mysterious flying object ceases to be easily recognizable. It may be an animal or a spirit or an alien or god—it no longer resembles a car at all.

2

Jane Smiley on What It's Like to Have Your Book Banned

In Conversation with Tai Caputo in the Iowa City High School Student Paper

Tai Caputo

Tai Caputo: As you may have heard, your Pulitzer Prizewinning novel, *A Thousand Acres*, has been banned from Iowa City Public Schools by the ICCSD because it contains "descriptions or depictions of sex acts."

This means that the book is not allowed to be in ICCSD classrooms or libraries. As the book's author, what is your opinion of this decision?

Jane Smiley: As I remember—and it's been a long time since I wrote it—I didn't actually depict any sex acts. I referred to one. And so, what can I say? I don't think banning *A Thousand Acres* is a very good idea, since the novel talks about a lot of other issues, and they're all from the female perspective. And those kinds of issues that are in the book—not just sex—such as domination, how to get around what your dad wants to do that you don't think is fair—those things are educational for students.

I think that if a mother or a father doesn't want their child to read a particular book, it's up to the mother or father to say, "No, honey, you can't read this right now, maybe later." It's not up to the state to decide who gets to read what.

I also wonder if it's being banned in Iowa because it's set in northern Iowa and it's also a critique of farming as it was changing in northern Iowa. So it occurs to me that maybe that's part of the reason for banning it.

TC: *A Thousand Acres* is set on an Iowa farm, but the story is based on Shakespeare's tragedy, *King Lear*. We read *King Lear* in AP Literature this year. In your opinion, what are the most adult themes and scenes in *King Lear*, and do you think your book contains more mature content than the Shakespeare play?

JS: The big question in *King Lear* is: why are Goneril and Regan at such odds with their dad when Cordelia isn't? And in that conflict, we're supposed to sympathize with Lear. But when I was growing up and reading King Lear and then when I decided to write the book, what I wanted was for Goneril and Regan to get to express their ideas, opinions, and feelings. There's a lot of soliloquies by Lear in the play, so he talks all the time.

But whatever Goneril and Regan did, I wanted to know why they did it and what they thought about it. So that was the point I was making when I was writing *A Thousand Acres*: that the women, the daughters, had their own point of view, and that their point of view was equally important as the father's point of view. The other thing is that there had to be a reason that Goneril, and especially Regan, were so hostile toward their dad.

Shakespeare rewrote a lot of previous material, so when I was looking up the previous material that he used to write *King Lear*, there was some suggestion that the king had violated his daughters, which was not uncommon in those days. And so I thought that would be an interesting and believable motive for the way that Ginny and Rose feel about their father.

TC: You lived in Iowa and taught at Iowa State for years. How many years did you live in Iowa, and how has Iowa changed since you lived here?

JC: Well, I moved to Iowa in September of 1972 and I was at the University of Iowa until I got my degree—I went to Iceland for a year too—so I came back, and kept studying there, and then I got a job at Iowa State, I think, in 1980. And then I was at Iowa State until '97. So I lived in Iowa for 25 years. I'd grown up in Missouri, in St. Louis, but I'd never been to Iowa before, and I found it really fascinating for a lot of reasons. I also thought Iowa City was much different from Ames, and I thought that was interesting.

So I enjoyed living there and I enjoyed the issues that were there. But politically, in those days, Iowa was a more liberal state than it is now. As I remember, there would be one Democratic senator and one Republican senator, and there was a sense that people had their opinions, but they got along. I do not know much about what's going on in Iowa now, but from the distance that I am, I understand that it's moved very much to the right, and that not only surprises me, it surprises my older daughter, who loved Iowa and thought Iowa was kind of a politically perfect spot. So we were both surprised that it shifted like that.

TC: You are also a parent of four children, some of whom were raised in Iowa. As a parent, do you think most high school students can handle the material in *A Thousand Acres*?

JS: I think that's an interesting question. I think seniors and juniors can handle it. I don't know about younger students, but that depends on the sort of books that the kids already read, both in school and on their own. I remember we had to read a Charles Dickens book when I was in 7th grade, and I (a) didn't understand it, and (b) couldn't understand how cruel people were in the book. But it opened my eyes to the era that Dickens was writing in. And we had to read another one in 8th grade, and then in 9th grade we read *David Copperfield*.

I got used to Dickens and his writing style, so when I read David Copperfield, I really embraced it. I loved it, I thought it was inspiring, and it taught me that not everybody in the world and in history has had the good luck that I had when I was a child in St. Louis and when

I lived in Iowa. And I think that's really important for kids. I think that kids need to find their way out into the world, and one way to find it is by reading novels and other books.

If you don't allow kids to open themselves up, then they won't understand things when they grow up, or even when they're, say, in college or in their late teens. They won't understand what's going on, or the reasons behind what their friends are doing. They won't understand how families differ, and it's really important that they read all kinds of books, so that they can get into the minds of all kinds of different people.

When I was growing up, I came from an extremely happy and agreeable family. But one of the things I loved, starting when I was in junior high, was Agatha Christie mysteries. I had never known anybody who'd been murdered or attacked, or anything like that, but I loved reading those mysteries. I probably read four or five of them a year. I learned a lot from them.

So I guess the question is, if you don't want your children to learn about bad things that happen around the world, are you going to not let them read the books that were written by one of the most popular authors in modern history? Are you going to stop them from reading, you know, murder mysteries, which is a popular genre? Are you going to stop them from going to movies where bad things happen? I think that's a bad idea. They have to learn.

TC: Your publisher, Penguin Random House, has filed a lawsuit against the State of Iowa to block the ban on all books from Iowa's K-12 schools that contain descriptions or depictions of sex acts and to have that portion of the law declared unconstitutional for violating the

First and Fourteenth Amendments of the US Constitution. What is your opinion of Penguin Random House's decision to file this lawsuit?

JS: Well, I didn't know they had filed a lawsuit. I think it should be the sort of thing that is worked out in courts. There should be these lawsuits. But there should also be attention to these lawsuits in newspapers, so that people can talk about them and have their opinions about them.

If there's anything we have in the US that I think is really good, it is constant conversation about what is right, what is wrong, what should be allowed, what shouldn't be allowed. Now, one of the things we know about banned books is that for many banned books that improves the sales of the book. And the reason is that as soon as you tell someone, especially someone who is young, that they aren't allowed to know a particular thing, then that person wants to know what it is. That person is curious and wants to know why he or she can't know about that particular thing.

Let's use a different example. Let's say that I lived near a polluted river. And my city did not allow any information about what was in the polluted river to be in the papers, to be in the news, to be on the internet. And yet, people in my city were getting ill and dying at a much higher rate than people who lived away from the river. Is my city going to justify those deaths by refusing to let anybody know how the river is being polluted? I think that's a similar issue.

TC: Some of us at City High are struggling to find reading material at school these days. Recently, ICCSD Director of Curriculum, Instruction, and Assessment, Carmen Gwenigale-Ogoli, communicated a policy to ICCSD teachers that K-12 students are not allowed to read any books brought from home for their English classes.

The school library's budget was not designed to cover such a wider range of reading material. What should we do? Do you have any reading advice for other Iowa public high school students?

JS: Order used books online. They're cheap, and you can have whatever you want. Talk about them amongst yourselves. You don't have to restrict reading to your English class. If you have a group of friends, you can form your own little book club and read them yourselves.

TC: I registered for a contemporary literature class this spring assuming I'd be allowed to bring books from home, and have just learned I am only allowed to read books from the school library. I had been planning to continue my personal research from a class last year in which I'd read 10 novels including *The Haunting of Hill House*, *Beloved*, and *Wuthering Heights*.

I brought a lot of my books for that project from home. The school library doesn't have *The Haunting of Hill House* or *Wuthering Heights*. I am interested in reading more books for this project in English and in French, but I won't be able to continue. What would you advise?

JS: They don't have *Wuthering Heights*? How could they possibly not have *Wuthering Heights*?

Part of the reason we do any project is so that we can understand what we're talking about. So if I were you, I would finish the project, and I would ask some of your friends to read it, and I would maybe even ask your teacher to have a look at it, just to see what they think, because a lot of teachers don't agree with these rules.

But I think your project sounds really interesting, and I think you should continue with it, because every project you do, whether it's writing nonfiction or an essay or fiction, is a way of understanding something. So I think you should continue with it and understand it, and then maybe in college or something you can turn it in. But I wouldn't stop it.

Here's what I always say as a writer: the first person you write for is yourself. And the reason you write for yourself is because you're learning things from what you're writing. When I was writing *A Thousand Acres*, the main thing I was learning about was not just family life, but agriculture. The history of agriculture and the way things changed, what it was like in the late 80s and early 90s, and what it meant.

That was fascinating to me, and I also thought it was really important, because basically the poisons going into the wells in northern Iowa were very dangerous, and so I learned a lot, from writing *A Thousand Acres*, about agriculture; and then when I wrote *The Last Hundred Years* trilogy I explored those issues over a longer time scale because that trilogy started in 1920 and ended in 2020. Those are issues, agricultural issues are ones that should be very much observed by people who happen to be eating food. And that was one of the reasons I wrote both of those, *A Thousand Acres* and *The Last Hundred Years* trilogy. So you learn about something, and you tell what you learned to somebody else, and that's the point. So even if they won't allow you to write that piece that you want to write, I would go ahead and write it. You'll learn from it, and you can show it to other people, and they can learn from it, too. I wouldn't stop.

TC: Do you think high school students should be protected from books containing descriptions of sexual acts?

JS: [Laughs] You can say that my response was to laugh out loud. Protecting students from books containing sexual acts does not protect them from performing sexual acts. And reading books about them teaches them how to connect, how to do it respectfully. What can I say?

Eventually, all kids, high school and college, have to learn about what it means to fall in love, to have sex, to have a partner, to get married, all that stuff. If you prevent them from learning about that, then they won't know how to do it, or they won't know how to go about it properly, in an honorable and respectful and affectionate way. They're going to learn about it anyway, so you just have to let them learn.

3

Keep Kids Reading

Carol Weston

I was once banned because of a book.

A school in Texas invited me down for an author visit. I'd been an advice columnist at *Girls' Life Magazine* since 1994, and had appeared on *Oprah* and *The Today Show* because of my books and bylines. I love talking to students about reading and writing. I tell them that as a kid, I was not a bookworm, but now, I love to read. And I encourage them to keep diaries because it's a wonderful way to develop their writing style and get to know themselves.

Knopf had just published my ninth book, *The Diary of Melanie Martin.* Melanie is ten, Matt the Brat is six, and their mom is an art teacher. But what their mom does *not* know is that when they go to museums and she rhapsodizes about Vermeer or van Gogh or Velázquez, Melanie and Matt play a secret game, Point Out the Naked People. And try not to giggle.

A fun and funny way to get kids into art and reading, right?

Well, a Dallas parent didn't think so, and boom, my visit got canceled.

Me? A bad influence?? I was shocked, but I let it go.

Three years and many author visits later, a Bronx public school asked if I'd speak to their fourth grade, pro-bono. In person, not on Zoom. A softie, I said yes. I even asked a philanthropic bibliophile if he'd donate 60 hardcover copies of *With Love from Spain, Melanie Martin*, the third novel in my series. I told him that these kids might not all have books at home. A softie, he said yes.

In the middle of my talk, I asked one of my go-to questions. "*¿Hay alguien aquí que hable español*?" Does anyone here speak Spanish? Eyes went wide and hands shot up. I told those kids how lucky they were to be bilingual from the get-go. It's a perspective they don't hear enough. Several children beamed—melting my heart.

After the talk, I took out my signing pen. The principal rushed over. "You can't give them books," he said.

"Excuse me?"

"What if parents object? I could lose my job."

This time I stood tall (not easy at 5'2") and said, "Won't they object if they find out you *didn't* let them have a free signed book?"

Flummoxed, the principal backed down, and I proceeded to autograph every copy, careful to spell each name correctly and glad to talk to the kids one-on-one.

But on the subway home, instead of reveling in the usual author-visit afterglow, I was stewing. Did that principal truly believe he had to protect his students (and their parents) from my paragraphs and pages? What a misuse of handwringing and outrage, especially since we should be doing all we can to help kids learn to love reading.

It's disheartening that so many books are met with stop signs, including classics that have made me a better, more empathetic person. *The Catcher in the Rye; The Lord of the Flies; 1984; The Color Purple; Beloved; Giovanni's Room; Brave New World; Are You There God, It's Me, Margaret; Maus; March; The Kite Runner; Fun Home; The Hate U Give; Madame Bovary; Doctor Zhivago.* Even *To Kill a Mockingbird*, for heaven's sake.

In eighth grade, I had copied down Atticus Finch's words: "You never really understand a person until you consider things from his point of view … until you climb inside of his skin and walk around in it." Compassion 101. And isn't climbing inside someone else's skin precisely what books make possible? Isn't understanding others an excellent argument for reading widely?

It makes me wistful to think back on those midnight *Harry Potter* launch parties: kids in capes lined up to buy and devour doorstoppers. Parents were proud, booksellers were over-the-moon, and no one got infected by black magic.

Philip Pullman's *His Dark Materials* was another blockbuster that faced fearful small-minded critics. Librarians were told to pull books from shelves. My husband had already read the first volume to our daughter; Lizzi finished the rest of the trilogy on her own. Decades later, she named her daughter after its heroine, Lyra.

Our Lyra is now six months old. Tonight, we bathed her in our kitchen sink as she splashed and cooed. I hope she'll grow up to love books. And I hope nonreaders won't tell her what she can and cannot read. If parents want to limit their children's choices, fine. But hands off my grandkids' bedside books.

I take solace in the words of author Katherine Applegate: "if somebody tells you *not* to read a book, that is a really good reason to head straight to the library." And I hope I can continue my mission of turning kids into readers—both mine and yours. Because kids who discover the joy and knowledge found in books have a better chance of growing up to be thoughtful and informed neighbors, parents, and voters.

And we're all in this together, aren't we?

4

From *U.S.!: A Novel*

Chris Bachelder

Chris Bachelder's 2006 novel considers the fates of the American left by constructing an imagined history in which muckraking novelist and 1934 candidate for governor of California Upton Sinclair's corpse is serially reanimated by idealistic young leftists and, once reanimated, serially killed by right-wing assassins. The novel climaxes in a small southern town, where the Greenville Anti-Socialist League is planning another Fourth of July book burning, this year of Sinclair's latest novel, A Moveable Jungle! *A significant part of this section of the novel is the story of the boy who volunteers to organize the burning; it's from this part of the book that the below excerpts are drawn.*[1]

The GASL Fourth of July Book Burning had at one time been an important social event in the town. People Arthur's age and older fondly remembered the raging bonfires of their youth. The mountain of gas-soaked books, garlanded with sparklers and strings

---

[1]Chris Bachelder, *U.S.! A Novel.* New York: Bloomsbury USA, 2006. Reproduced with permission.

of firecrackers, burning deep into the summer night. The children, permitted to stay up late for this one special night, dancing circles around the inferno of leftist literature. The burning, however, had fallen off in recent years. Three years ago it had been cancelled by rain, and the last two years nobody in the league had even bothered with it. But then the previous January old Miller Ames died and left the GASL some of his money, a significant portion of which he earmarked for book burning. It was his wish that the event return to its former glory and significance. Oh, did Miller Ames hate Socialism! You just don't see that kind of fervor much these days.

[…]

Stephen stood on the bench and clutched his inhaler, trying to keep his knees from shaking, trying not to scratch at his neck or dig in his ears. The senior citizens at his table stared up at him and clapped. Arthur, visibly proud of his son, called for a vote. All in favor raised their hands and held them high, Nancy stood and began to count but there was no need. The majority was overwhelming, the will of the people was clear. In this way it was decided that young Stephen Rudkin was in charge of the Greenville Anti-Socialist League Fourth of July Book Burning.

[…]

Stephen could not sleep on the eve of the book burning. He lay beneath only a sheet in his narrow bed, going through his checklist over and over again. In the garage he had the five gas cans, filled. He had a twenty-five-foot length of rope to use as a wick. He had yellow CAUTION tape to mark off the bonfire area. He had the firecrackers and the sparklers. He had a fire extinguisher and safety goggles. He had arranged with Myron Lewis for a big off-season delivery of firewood, which would give the pile structural support and a long-lasting center. (He had called Myron that morning to make sure Myron was prepared; he would call again the next morning, he decided.) And of course he had the books, five hundred Upton Sinclair titles, shipped directly to his front door from Red Shovel Press. Stephen had feared the books would not arrive in time. He had had nightmares of showing up at the burning, in front of the entire town, with two of his school notebooks and a green stick he pulled off of a tree. He had grown despondent, desperate. He paced the house, close to tears. He ran outside, night or day, when he heard a truck on the street. His father told him not to worry, though Arthur himself had become a bit concerned when the books had not arrived by the first of July. But they had come the morning of the second: fifteen boxes. Now Stephen lay in bed and thought of the books, arranged in four stacks along a wall in the dark garage. Fifteen boxes of Socialist propaganda in his own garage! Three stacks of four boxes and one stack of three. It was thrilling and terrifying to consider the number and proximity of those dangerous books. Yesterday Stephen had bought a second padlock for the garage door. He had considered whether to charge the four-dollar padlock to the GASL book-burning account, but in the end he decided the padlock was an extraneous expense, and he paid for it himself with his own lawn-mowing money.

Gas, rope, CAUTION tape, fireworks, fire extinguisher, safety goggles, firewood, books. Stephen had his book-burning clothes laid out on top of his pine dresser with his inhaler. It was best, the Internet articles agreed, not to wear anything long, baggy, or loose-fitting, such as bathrobes, ponchos, dresses, sarongs, or trench coats. To the best of his knowledge Stephen did not own any of these items; in fact, most of his clothes were uncomfortably snug after his recent growth spurt. He laid out the snuggest: jeans and a year-old striped shirt.

Gas, rope, CAUTION tape, fireworks, fire extinguisher, safety goggles, firewood, books, clothes. He also had instructions, printed from the Internet, for how to construct the book pile to achieve your desired effect. There was quick-burn methodology and slow-burn methodology. Many people (including Stephen, just a week ago!) assumed that you simply dumped your books on the ground and lit a match. You could do this, of course, but don't your friends and neighbors deserve better? There were very specific ways to create beautiful, safe, and memorable book burnings, specifically suited to your unique celebration. The arrangement of books and firewood and other flammable material was vital, as was the amount and application of gasoline, as was the wick mechanism. Why not create a book burning that is most appropriate to the mood of your occasion? (If you are unsure of the type of book burning you're looking for, turn to Worksheet 3 and take the short quiz.)

Stephen had done the research by himself on the lone computer in the Greenville Public Library. He had asked Mrs. Middleton for help—he had asked her three times, in fact. The first two times she told him she was busy and Stephen waited patiently. It was not like her to ignore him or put him off. They were friends, after all. When he approached the third time, Mrs. Middleton sighed and said, "Stephen, honey, what if we searched for something else? I'll show you how to use a search engine and I'll teach you how to get around the Internet, but not help you look up how to burn books. Is that OK?"

Stephen shrugged. "I guess so," he said. "But why?"

Mrs. Middleton asked Stephen to look around him. "I have," she said, "a certain professional regard for books, regardless of their content." That sentence stuck in Stephen's brain. It was an elegant sentence, regardless of its content. Mrs. Middleton, whose quavering speech at the GASL meeting still had people in town rolling their eyes, was emerging in Stephen's mind as an eccentric. They sat together and searched the Internet for sled dogs, Benjamin Franklin, and the lost city of Atlantis. Stephen was a quick learner and when left on his own, he quickly found dozens of sites on book burning. He selected the most comprehensive, highly regarded site (linked at Bewaretheldes) and printed it after Mrs. Middleton reluctantly showed him how to use the printer. Those pages, now stapled and filled with Stephen's marginalia and underline marks, lay on the pine dresser next to his clothes and his inhaler.

Stephen was wide awake. The weather forecast was good. It was very good. The forecast had been good all week and it was still good. Sunny and hot. From time to time he thought he felt something crawling across his foot or leg. He tried to concentrate on his checklist, which was not difficult.

Gas, rope, CAUTION tape, fireworks, fire extinguisher, safety goggles, firewood, books, clothes, instructions. There was, in addition to these items, Stephen's speech, which was handwritten on paper torn from a spiral notebook. Stephen did not want to give a speech and he had no specific reason to expect that he would have to. But he had, on occasion, attended functions at which someone, and once his father, was asked to give a speech. Not asked, really. Implored. "Speech!" people yelled. "Speech!" And the person singled out had to stand up and give a speech. Stephen could recall the terror he had felt on the speaker's behalf. If as the director of this year's book burning, Stephen was asked to give a speech—if his neighbors and teachers began chanting "Speech!"—Stephen wanted to be prepared. The short speech, hidden in the top drawer of the dresser, was little more than a compilation of his father's favorite sayings and lessons, culled from the dinner table and the couch, about human nature, competition, hard work, and the survival of the fittest. The speech ended with Arthur's favorite homily: *Look out the window.* (Stephen did not write *window* because the book burning would be outside.) *Take a good look out there. The squirrels are chasing each other around the tree. The ants are hauling away the carcass of the beetle. The birds are stealing each other's nests. This is our natural world. Socialism ain't natural.* (After lengthy consideration, Stephen kept the ain't. He knew it was wrong, but he felt intuitively that it was forceful and persuasive. He hoped his English teacher would understand.)

Stephen got out of bed when he realized there was no use trying to sleep. This was worse than Christmas Eve. He turned on a football helmet lamp and checked the items on top of the dresser, then opened the top drawer to see his folded speech. He turned off his lamp and left the bedroom in his white underwear, sidestepping in the dark hallway a bucket that was a quarter full of old rainwater. His father slept shirtless on the couch in front of the television. The cushions were worn and soft, and Arthur's body sagged deep into the couch, as if he were in a hammock. The windows were open and a rattling box fan blew warm air into the room. Stephen turned off the television and removed the empty glass that rested precariously on the arm of the couch by his father's head.

In the kitchen he took a flashlight from a drawer because the fluorescent lights in the garage took forever to come on. He unlocked the door and opened it as quietly as he could. He imagined, with the terrible force of a nightmare, that the four stacks of books would be missing from the garage. His breath came short and he had to stop in order to concentrate. His inhaler was back in his room, and he didn't want to return for it. He thought about sled dogs to settle down. When you typed *sled dogs* into a search engine, a world opened up. His breathing returned to normal and he entered the garage, which smelled strongly of gas. The books were there, against the wall, next to the gas and other supplies. Or at least the book boxes were there. He walked across the gritty floor on tiptoes and inspected the boxes, which seemed to still contain the books. He felt nervous to be alone in the dark with books that were so wrong they had to be destroyed. The smell of the gas made him lightheaded and giddy. He pointed the flashlight at the shipping label on the side of a box: *Red Shovel Press. A Moveable Jungle! Upton Sinclair*. He tried to open a box, but he couldn't remove the heavy tape. The other boxes appeared to be similarly taped, so he put the flashlight on top of the box, picked it up, and carried it back into the house. The box was heavier than he expected it to be.

In his room, with the door shut and the lamp on, Stephen used the key to the new padlock to saw through the packing tape, stopping once to use his inhaler. On the quiet count of three he jerked open the flaps of the box, half expecting to see something horrible inside. A dead animal or a severed limb. But what he saw, when he opened his eyes, was just an invoice slip on top of stacks of identical paperback books. Stephen got up and checked to see if his door was locked. It was. He unlocked it and locked it again, then returned to the box on the floor.

He cautiously picked one of the books from the box, once more expecting a nasty surprise, a burn or a shock, but the book felt normal in his hands. He looked at the cover of *A Moveable Jungle!*, an image of two powerful arms clasping each other. There were no people, no bodies, just these muscular arms, linked. It was like a handshake, except the hands gripped the forearms, just beneath the elbows. The arms were drawn, not photographed. They were realistic, but the muscles and the creases in the rolled-up sleeves seemed stylized and exaggerated, like the figures in comic books.

Years later he would vividly remember this night, sitting in his white underwear on the floor of his room, holding *A Moveable Jungle!*, perched at the edge of something vast. He would say, later, that he had intended to build a miniature model of the book pile in his room. He would say he had intended to practice his burning technique, and this may have been true. It probably was. But instead of building the model pile, Stephen held the book in his hands, turning it over and over. He felt the sharp corner of the cover with his index finger and he flipped the crisp pages with his thumb. He lifted the book to his nose and inhaled as deeply as his anxious breathing allowed. He opened to the middle, closed his eyes, and buried his face in the crease, inhaling. The smell of the novel! Beneath the mild sweetness of the pages he detected the medicinal, antiseptic scent of the ink, the chemical tang of the glue. The object in Stephen's hands seemed to belong to some new and distinct category, some new species of object, not even distantly related to the soft-cornered, water-stained, dog-eared volumes at the town library or to the bleached and battered textbooks at his school. Stephen, it should be said, had never held a new book. Instead of building his miniature pile in preparation for the GASL book burning, he opened the novel to the first page and began reading, and he did not stop until he had finished it. By that time the sun was coming up on the Fourth of July and for Stephen the world was a very different place.

[...]

Stephen had slept only three hours, and when he awoke on the floor with the novel on his chest, he found that nothing in his life was the same. He felt that the book had been a strange dream and that he was still trapped within it. Before getting dressed that morning, he read the Labels on his clothes. The people who made them were like him and his father. One was a shy young girl, Stephen's age, with shiny hair. She made Stephen's shirt because her family needed the money. Everyone in her family worked hard, and yet nothing good came of it. It was awful what they suffered and what they lost. It was not fair—this was the childish but bone-hard truth that Stephen could not dismiss or assimilate, not now and not in the disobedient years to come. This was the beginning and the end of a political philosophy. He could have been her and she could have been him. Stephen had stood at his bedroom window that morning and prayed a selfish prayer for rain. He had actually put his hands together and closed his eyes. He figured he had a better chance to influence the weather than the global economy, though here now was the bright sun, the cloudless holiday sky.

Overnight, everything had changed—his father, his hometown, the GASL. Every article in every section of the Greenville *Echo* looked different today, the Fourth of July, than it would have the day before. Even the sports and human interest stories. But it was Upton Sinclair and his novel that had changed the most. The thought of burning even one copy of *A Moveable Jungle!*, much less five hundred, made Stephen sick to his stomach.

PART TWO

ARGUMENTS ABOUT BOOK BANNING

5

Why Americans Must Speak Up to Defend Educational Autonomy

Jeremy C. Young and Jacqueline Allain

"We aren't always for diversity."

"The world needs more cowboys … not more social justice warriors."

"DEI must die."

These quotes are not from Internet trolls, or from authoritarian governments in places such as Hungary or Russia. They are from legislators in Kentucky, Wyoming, and Nebraska who are seeking to undermine diversity and free inquiry at US colleges and universities.[1]

A version of this essay was first published as "Why Americans Must Speak Up to Defend University Autonomy," at University World News on March 15, 2024, https://www.universityworldnews.com/post.php?story=20240315104751579.

[1] Hannah Pinski, "'We Aren't Always for Diversity.' Kentucky Senate Advances Limits on DEI Programs," *Louisville Courier Journal*, February 13, 2024, https://www.courier-journal.com/story/news/politics/2024/02/13/senate-bill-6-limiting-diversity-programs-at-kentucky-colleges-advances/72589142007/; Maya Shimizu Harris, "Wyoming Lawmakers

In these states and others, Americans are witnessing a proliferation of legislation that effectively demolishes academic freedom and institutional autonomy at colleges and universities. Together, these bills place American higher education in grave peril.

The solution, we believe, is for American higher education leaders, and the public at large, to embrace both academic freedom and a concept that has thus far been far more influential in Europe than in the United States: the autonomy of universities from direct political interference.

As of March 2025, over 230 laws or policies restricting higher education have been introduced in 38 US states since 2021. Though the majority have not passed, state governments have enacted 25 laws or policies in 17 states that directly undermine academic freedom and university autonomy.[2]

This higher education legislation has been matched by laws and policies restricting K-12 schools, most notably by a stark rise in school book bans at the K-12 level.[3] From July 2023 to June 2024, PEN America's Index of School Book Bans recorded 10,046 instances of book bans across 29 states and 220 public school districts.[4] When

---

Set for Showdown over UW Gender Studies, Diversity Office," *WyoFile*, February 21, 2024, https://wyofile.com/wyoming-lawmakers-set-for-showdown-over-uw-gender-studies-diversity-office/; Emily Marin, "'DEI Must Die': Nebraska Bill Would Ban University Diversity Pledges," *The College Fix*, March 8, 2024, https://www.thecollegefix.com/dei-must-die-nebraska-bill-would-ban-university-diversity-pledges/.

[2]PEN America, "PEN America Index of Educational Gag Orders," Spreadsheet, n.d., https://airtable.com/appg59iDuPhlLPPFp/shrtwubfBUo2tuHyO/tblZ40w5HLBuTK9vs/viw5lFPxKHGkamF0k?blocks=hide.

[3]Kasey Meehan et al., "Banned in the USA: Beyond the Shelves," Banned in the USA (PEN America, November 1, 2024), https://pen.org/report/beyond-the-shelves/.

[4]PEN America, "PEN America Index of School Book Bans—2023-2024," Table, 2024, https://pen.org/book-bans/pen-america-index-of-school-book-bans-2023-2024/.

taken all together, between July 2021 and June 2024, the organization recorded 15,940 instances of book bans across 43 states and 415 public school districts.

As consistently documented since the first report in 2021, book bans continue to deliberately target specific themes, content areas, and representations. Book bans overwhelmingly affect books about race and racism, LGBTQ+ people and characters, people and characters of color, and books with sex-related content.

The higher education restrictions have been much the same story. The first wave of bills, in 2021 and 2022, took the form of what PEN America calls educational gag orders: legislation that directly censors educational speech, usually in the classroom.[5] This legislation, frequently described by its proponents as "anti-Critical Race Theory" bills, focused on banning a list of so-called "divisive concepts" related to race, gender, identity, and United States history. These bills culminated with Florida's "Stop WOKE Act," whose implementation was stayed by a federal court in November 2022 on constitutional grounds.[6]

Lawmakers responded by changing tactics. Beginning in 2023 and escalating in the 2024 state legislative sessions, a growing number of bills have focused not on direct censorship of faculty members' academic freedom, but instead on a kind of *indirect* effort to suppress academia, restricting various aspects of university governance, including the approval of general education curricula, the creation

---

[5] Jonathan Friedman and James Tager, "Educational Gag Orders: Legislative Restrictions on the Freedom to Read, Learn, and Teach" (PEN America, November 8, 2021), https://pen. org/report/educational-gag-orders/.

[6] Mark E. Walker, Pernell v. Florida Board of Governors of the State University System (United States District Court, Northern District of Florida, Tallahassee Division, November 17, 2022).

or suspension of degree programs, faculty tenure policies, university mission statements, accreditation agencies, and the right of a university to maintain an office or initiative that promotes diversity, equity, or inclusion (DEI) initiatives. Bills restricting DEI and other aspects of university governance have already become law in Florida, Texas, North Carolina, and Utah, and appear headed for passage in several other states.[7]

This effort by elected officials to assert ideological control over university governance is a relatively new phenomenon in the United States. But it is far more common elsewhere in the world, including by authoritarian governments in Russia, China, and Hungary, and former governments in Poland and Brazil.[8] In particular, it echoes Hungarian prime minister Viktor Orbán's 2018 censorship of gender studies programs and expulsion of Central European University.[9]

It's time for American higher education leaders to respond to these threats the way higher education leaders in other countries have responded: by emphasizing the importance of university autonomy for intellectual freedom.[10]

---

[7]Jeffrey Adam Sachs and Jeremy C. Young, "America's Censored Classrooms 2023: Lawmakers Shift Strategies as Resistance Rises," America's Censored Classrooms (PEN America, November 9, 2023), https://pen.org/report/americas-censored-classrooms-2023/.
[8]Nadine Farid Johnson, "The US Is Inspiring Education Censorship Elsewhere," *Al Jazeera*, January 4, 2023, https://www.aljazeera.com/opinions/2023/1/4/the-us-is-exporting-education-censorship-2.
[9]Jeremy C. Young, "Christopher Rufo's Alarming and Deceptive Crusade Against Public Universities," *TIME*, August 30, 2023, https://time.com/6309612/christopher-rufo-public-universities-deceptive-essay/.
[10]Jeremy C. Young, "PEN America Endorses the Magna Charta Universitatum 2020," pen.org, October 9, 2024, https://pen.org/pen-america-endorses-the-magna-charta-universitatum-2020/.

For nearly forty years, global higher education leaders have recognized that the autonomy of universities from direct ideological control by politicians is paramount to academic freedom. According to the Magna Charta Universitatum, a 1988 statement (revised in 2020) signed by nearly a thousand universities across the world, "Intellectual and moral autonomy is the hallmark of any university and a precondition for the fulfilment of its responsibilities to society."[11] The European University Association maintains an Autonomy Scorecard that evaluates whether universities in the various European countries can operate without ideological interference from elected officials.[12]

Unfortunately, while there is a robust tradition of protections for academic freedom in the United States, there is not a similarly strong tradition of concern for institutional autonomy.[13] Too many people agree with Christopher Rufo, one of the major architects of the anti-education legislation we are seeing in the US, who has said that: "Public universities are public institutions, governed by state legislatures and funded by taxpayers. Their institutional autonomy is a privilege granted by voters, not a right guaranteed by the Constitution."[14]

---

[11]"Magna Charta Universitatum 2020" (Magna Charta Observatory, March 12, 2020), https://www.magna-charta.org/magna-charta-universitatum/mcu2020.

[12]"University Autonomy in Europe IV: The Scorecard 2023" (European University Association, March 7, 2023), https://www.eua.eu/publications/reports/university-autonomy-in-europe-iv-the-scorecard-2023.html.

[13]American Association of University Professors, "1940 Statement of Principles on Academic Freedom and Tenure" (American Association of University Professors, 1940), https://www.aaup.org/report/1940-statement-principles-academic-freedom-and-tenure; Timothy Reese Cain, "Accreditation, Academic Freedom, and Institutional Autonomy: Historical Precedents and Modern Imperatives," *AAUP Journal of Academic Freedom* 14 (2023): 12.

[14]Christopher F. Rufo, "D.E.I. Programs Are Getting in the Way of Liberal Education," *New York Times*, July 27, 2023, https://www.nytimes.com/2023/07/27/opinion/christopher-rufo-diversity-desantis-florida-university.html.

Rufo's position betrays a fundamental misunderstanding of public institutions. Taxpayers might pay for a public park, but they do not determine who has access to it. Similarly, public universities are places where all ideas can be debated and get a fair hearing, free from ideological control by the government. A university that lacks this sort of political autonomy is not a university at all.

The ongoing assault on academic freedom and institutional autonomy in the United States will only end when Americans speak up in defense of academic freedom, university autonomy, and the democratic mandate of higher education. It's never been a better time to start.

6

From the Word to the World

Emily Drabinski

Donnelly, Idaho, has a lot in common with other rural communities in this country. An economy that had been based around lumber, mining, and ranching has turned toward tourism as those industries fade. The opioid epidemic has ravaged families, leaving many children in single-parent households where ends can't always be made to meet. A worsening climate has made life even harder; just this September, Donnelly became a refuge for neighbors in surrounding Valley County, driven from their homes by the deadly Line Fire.

In 2018, Laura Bettis teamed up with Sherry Scheline, a fifth-generation resident of the area, to build Donnelly its own library. A small log cabin that can fit just fifteen people, Donnelly Public Library quickly became the heart of the town. Scheline purchased a bounce house and cotton candy machine that anyone could check out. In a town where more than 40% of families live below the federal poverty line, any child can enjoy a stupendous birthday party. When she learned that Donnelly had no after school options for working families, she started a library club open to all where children could head after the final bell while their parents could be assured of their safety. Miss Sherry would always take care of them. And once a month, Scheline held an after-hours gathering for trans and gender-expansive youth in the area. Just a handful of kids showed up each month to eat pizza and comply with Scheline's only rule for the group: in order to participate, you must be reading a book. For those few children, that hour each month was the only place they could use the names they had chosen for themselves and hear those names said by others.

Do you remember the first time you were acknowledged like this? Seen for what you suspected or feared you might be? What it meant to understand that you weren't alone in desiring what you desired, wanted what you wanted? How many of us discovered we were not alone in the pages of a book? For me, I was 20 years old, in college in the late 1990s, and it was Alison Bechdel's *Dykes to Watch Out For*. What book did this for you? Was it something by John Rechy or Christopher Isherwood? Dorian Gray or *Giovanni's Room*? I think I read *Rubyfruit Jungle* a dozen times.

There's a frame in Alison Bechdel's memoir *Fun Home* where she discovers her sexuality much the way many of us probably did: sprawled on a bed in her college dorm room, reading. Books are central to identity for so many of us. We read a book that helps us engage in that private negotiation of the self that we call coming out. And then we use those books to come out to each other. Have you read *Tales of the City?* is an invitation to join the social world where we can be ourselves, with and for each other.

Having found myself in books, I have made my life in books. I am a librarian.

Until 2021, I'll admit I envied young queer people for how many more stories they have access to than I did growing up. The flourishing of LGBTQIA+ literature has been amazing to watch, especially as a librarian who has spent my career selecting, acquiring, describing, shelving, circulating, and preserving books that fit into the HQ 76 spot on academic library shelves—that's the call number for our stories, where I have spent a lot of my time. But in 2021, we began to see an uptick in challenges to books like Maia Kobabe's *Gender Queer*, Jonathan Evison's *Lawn Boy*, *All Boys Aren't Blue* by George M. Johnson, *Melissa* by Alex Gino. The challenges were coordinated, highly organized, and cropping up everywhere from New York to California, Iowa to Idaho, Florida to Texas. The American Library Association reported the largest number of documented challenges in its history of reporting. In 2022, that number went up higher. In 2023 and 2024, even higher. And here we are in 2025. One of the first acts taken by the current presidential administration was to eliminate the position established by President Biden to investigate and address organized censorship in schools and libraries. Our book ban czar? Like so many federal workers, he was fired.

In the middle of this firestorm, I became the first openly LGBTQIA+ president in the nearly 150 year history of the American Library Association. (Definitely not the first; we know we have always been everywhere.) The attacks on books about who we are quickly became attacks on who I am. I took office in June 2023. In July, I listened in on a hearing of the Montana State Library Commission as it decided to cut its membership in ALA due to its president: me. Public comment included someone reading passages from Leviticus. My inbox and social media feeds filled with hate. Over the course of the year, three states would see legislation banning the use of public funds for anything ALA-related because of its president: me. A woman began following me around, screen recording online talks and even recording me at an event in Chicago, uploading videos complete with hateful commentary for a growing audience of extremists. Each week, staff at ALA would send me a compiled list of my appearances in extremist media where I was pilloried for my sexuality, my family, and my political beliefs.

And the attacks weren't limited to just me. Librarians in Alabama told me that not a week went by where they didn't get a harassing phone call from a community member demanding to know whether they were lesbians too. In Louisiana, my photo appeared on slide decks at local library board meetings, an example of the poison that is the American Library Association and, by extension, libraries themselves.

What happened to me is happening to librarians all across the country. I know this because I talked to hundreds of them during my year of service. Amanda Jones in Lafayette Parish, Louisiana, can't go to the grocery store without being attacked by members of her own community because of her support for the right to read. Kimber Glidden in Boundary County, Idaho, doesn't even work in libraries anymore. She was driven out by armed extremists who followed her and her staff home from work, calling them groomers. Glidden's library didn't even own any of the books that were on the list activists demanded be banned. Brooky Parks refused to cancel a library program directed at LGBTQIA+ youth of color and was fired from her job. A state librarian in a very blue state—this is happening everywhere—was placed on administrative leave pending an investigation into the distribution of child pornography after posting a photo on social media of herself holding Kobabe's *Gender Queer* with the caption, "My child and I are reading this book together so we can better understand who they are." And in a small town in Michigan, the library closed altogether after everyone on staff quit, no longer willing or able to contend with the hate directed at them for the simple fact that most of the staff was gay.

In 2024, these attacks hit Sherry Scheline and her small library in Donnelly. After three years of attacks by organized censorship groups bent on removing any evidence of LGBTQ+ and BIPOC history, literary production, and even our existence, Brad Little, the governor of Idaho, signed into law HB 710. This law requires librarians in Idaho to move books from the youth section to the adult section at the request of anyone who asks them to or risk a $250 fine. $250, an amount laughably small in relation to the state budget but the entire collections budget for many a library in America. Scheline cannot comply with this legislation. She can't move books to a different part of the library because Donnelly Public Library has only one room. In July, just weeks after the state law passed, she closed her library to anyone under 18 unless they came in with an adult or had written permission from their parents to be in the library alone. Those gay and lesbian stories that matter so much to us when we're young? That too many of us have to hide from our parents as we try to discover who we are outside of disciplinary view? Off limits, no matter how much Miss Sherry wants to share them.

The reality for librarians right now is that we are facing the same attacks so many of our LGBTQIA+ community members are facing.

Assaults on the right to read our stories are happening at the same time as attacks on gender affirming healthcare, access to organized sports in high schools, safe passage to public bathrooms, the right to be represented in school curricula. The facts of our very existence are in dispute and under pressure. Librarians like me are on the front lines of these struggles.

But as we know, there is always hope. My hope derives from the communities that are organizing to win the world we want. Communities like this one.

In 2022, Mel Manuel and Jeremy JF Thompson moved from New Orleans across Lake Pontchartrain to the Northshore. When they got there, they realized they needed LGBTQIA+ friends and they set out to make them like we always do. They started the social group Queer Northshore and got people together. Potlucks with plenty of lentil salads. Roller skating nights. Meetups at bars and at bookstores. And they mobilized this growing community to combat book banning efforts in St. Tammany Parish. When activists started pushing to remove books with LGBTQIA+ stories, Queer Northshore showed up, stacking library board meetings. They wrote letters and made phone calls, held rallies. Two years later, books are returning to the shelves of the library, emerging out from behind the desk and into the hands of readers who need them, readers like me. Mel ran for Congress in Louisiana's district one, challenging Steve Scalise, who has built his career in part on attacks against our communities. And Jeremy is now an elected delegate in the Louisiana Democratic party where they are organizing with others to put people who believe in libraries, who care about queer and trans people, into positions of political power in the south.

I heard dozens of stories like this one during my year as ALA president. I visited 31 states and seven countries, including a 4,951 mile road trip last June. We drove 4,951 miles in a van with a video camera, documenting the power of American libraries. Everywhere I went I met people fighting together for a world where all of us can be free. A school librarian in Llano County, Texas, refused to remove queer books from her library and was fired. She won a judgement against the county last month. A Connecticut selectman asked the Kent Memorial Library to remove a book about pronouns from a display. The library board followed their review policies and the book remained in place. And in Donnelly, Idaho, just last month, a coalition of publishers, authors, and library supporters filed suit against the state of Idaho on behalf of the people of Donnelly, each of whom has as much a right to read—and to be who they are—as any of us.

You don't need me to tell you we are living in dangerous times. As we always have, we will live and love and survive together, in part through the stories we tell. That means that as we fight for each other, we must also fight for our libraries. If you don't have a library card, go get one. If you have one, use it. Join the American Library Association's Show Up for Libraries campaign and add your voice to thousands of others who believe in these crucial public institutions.

And when things get tough, I encourage you to do what I do and turn off the world and find yourself the way queer people always have: in the pages of a book.

7

Is It Ever OK to Ban a Book?

Leonard Cassuto

The very phrase "banned books" suggests an absolute right to free speech for writers and their readers. I aim to complicate that stance, but before I do, I must confess my practical sympathy with it. As a citizen of a divided nation and a member of a besieged academic workplace, I don't agree with everything that I'm about to say. As a pragmatic matter, I value the absolute stance against banning books because every exception makes things more complicated— and complications can cause contortions, or worse. Nevertheless, absolutism involves some contortions of its own, and it has real costs. I mean to illuminate some of those here.

I

Let's start with the family. (The novelist and memoirist Pat Conroy once described a family as a "small civilization.")[1] Families routinely control information and sometimes ban it. Here's one common example: When a parent has cancer, they don't always tell their children right away. Sometimes they never tell them. You might support or reject that position, but I expect that we can agree that it's at least debatable.

Families also ban books, and movies and other media. Do you care about the age of your child when they first see (or read) *The Exorcist*? What about *The Cook, the Thief, His Wife, and Her Lover*? Maybe you do or maybe you don't, but reasonable people—some of whom are married to each other—may disagree about decisions like this. I don't know too many parents who allow their children unfettered access to all media at any age. And any exception is a crack in the seamless wall.

II

From the family, let's expand the field to the neighborhood. A recent letter to Kwame Anthony Appiah's *New York Times* "Ethicist" column described a local book-banning question. The writer runs a "Little Free Library" in their front yard from which "I encourage my neighbors to

---

[1] Pat Conroy, "Anatomy of a Divorce." *Atlanta Magazine*, November 1, 1978. https://www.atlantamagazine.com/great-reads/anatomy-of-a-divorce/.

take books and leave books." Recently, the writer explained, someone had been donating children's books advocating creationism to this common space. As someone who opposes both book banning and also advocating a creationist point of view to children (or anyone else), the writer wondered whether they are ethically obligated to distribute the creationist books.[2]

The writer is asking whether it's acceptable to ban from their local space books that argue for a point of view with which they strongly disagree. The threat, of course, is that children and other credulous characters will read these books and then agree with what they espouse. As the owner of the property upon which the book exchange stands, the writer surely has the power to ban the offending books from their space, but that's not the issue. Instead, they're asking whether it's the right thing to do.

Let us first acknowledge that this is a reasonable question. I doubt that many people who are reading this have a reflexive answer to it. It's an "on one hand" and "on the other hand" kind of question—and that's my point. Appiah, the professional ethicist, admits as much when he says that "the situation isn't so clear-cut when it comes to libraries meant for minors." Appiah further observes that "people who say that they're opposed to banning books often wish themselves to keep certain books off the school shelves," and local public librarians, who operate with limited budgets, are bound to purchase books that will

---

[2]Kwame Anthony Appiah, "Can I Ban Books from my Front-Yard Little Free Library?" *The New York Times*, January 19, 2025, 14–15. https://www.nytimes.com/2025/01/10/magazine/little-free-library-ethics.html.

appeal to the people who would use their public facilities.[3] While this doesn't exactly amount to banning certain books, it has a relatively similar effect.

All of this is to say that the question of whether to ban books to protect minors is already getting complicated. And we may further observe that outside of age-restricted senior communities, minors tend to be everywhere.

III

Now let's make the natural move from neighborhoods to societies. Consider Germany to start. Masha Gessen recently described how "Germany has long regulated the ways in which the Holocaust is remembered and discussed." Angela Merkel, when she was chancellor of Germany, called this regulation "part of Germany's *Staatsräson*—the reason for the existence of the state."[4]

Before we move to cases—and you may already anticipate one I have in mind—let's look closely at Merkel's statement, made in a speech to the Israeli Knesset in 2008. Merkel declared that "every federal government and every chancellor before me was committed to Germany's special historical responsibility for Israel's security." This

---

[3]It should also be mentioned that these questions have increased the pressure on local librarians in many communities. See, for example, Elizabeth A. Harris and Alexandra Alter, "With Rising Book Bans, Librarians Have Come Under Attack." *The New York Times*, July 6, 2022. https://www.nytimes.com/2022/07/06/books/book-ban-librarians.html.

[4]Masha Gessen, "In the Shadow of the Holocaust." *The New Yorker*, December 9, 2023. https://www.newyorker.com/news/the-weekend-essay/in-the-shadow-of-the-holocaust.

responsibility, rooted in history, Merkel said, is part of Germany's reason for being. It's a widely-scoped rationale for the banning of information that ironically locates its rationale in "a culture of remembrance that will endure even when the survivors of the Shoah are no longer with us."[5] Merkel locates her justification in history: because we should not forget the Holocaust, we should regulate information that might encourage people to forget it. Without marking any specific cases, Merkel argues on a moral basis that certain information should be suppressed in order to preserve the integrity of certain other information.

This strategy raises concerns, of course, starting with the question of who's making the choices about which information to preserve or suppress. Without an absolute stance that leads to mechanical decision-making, it will always be humans who make those choices—and one problem with humans is that they're human. But the rationale itself aims to promote social good.

Adolph Hitler's *Mein Kampf* was banned in Germany starting immediately after World War II. The book was kept in a physical vault and could be read by Germans only for documented scholarly reasons. (This practice came to an end when the book's copyright expired in 2016. At that point, the German government supported the production of a heavily-annotated edition by the Institute of Contemporary History of Munich (IfZ). That hefty volume remains the only edition of *Mein Kampf* that can be sold in Germany. The IfZ

---

[5]"Speech by Federal Chancellor Angela Merkel before the Knesset, March 18, 2008 in Jerusalem." https://www.bundesregierung.de/breg-de/service/bulletin/rede-von-bundeskanzlerin-dr-angela-merkel-796170.

edition sold 85,000 copies at a pricy 58 euros per copy during its first year of issue, making it a surprise bestseller.)[6]

The banning of *Mein Kampf* does not stand alone. Holocaust denial (and Nazi symbols and slogans) have been illegal in Germany since 1985. In 1985, Holocaust denial was banned as an insult to every Jew in Germany. But in 1994 the law was amended, and Holocaust denial (along with the symbols and slogans) were additionally classified as forms of incitement, and banned under anti-incitement law, with an increased penalty.[7] (Holocaust denial is also illegal in many other European countries. It's legal in the United States, but American courts have also established the Holocaust as a historical fact.)

As Gessen shows, the German antisemitism laws have led to some uncomfortable contradictions over time. Policing Holocaust denial—and antisemitism generally—has turned into a small bureaucracy in Germany, with "dozens of antisemitism commissioners" who "have no single job description or legal framework for their work." To Gessen, "much of it appears to consist of publicly shaming those they see as antisemitic, often for 'de-singularizing the Holocaust' or for criticizing Israel." The targets of this mobbing behavior have included a number of Jews.[8]

---

[6]"First Mein Kampf reprint in Germany since war set for sixth print run." *The Guardian*, January 7, 2017. https://www.theguardian.com/world/2017/jan/03/first-mein-kampf-reprint-germany-since-war-sixth-print-run-hitler.

[7]Michael J. Bazyler, "Holocaust Denial Laws and Other Legislation Criminalizing Promotion of Nazism." *Yad Vashem* https://www.yadvashem.org/holocaust/holocaust-antisemitism/holocaust-denial-laws.html.

[8]Gessen observes that "These have included the German-Israeli sociologist Moshe Zuckermann, who was targeted for supporting the B.D.S. movement, as was the South African Jewish photographer Adam Broomberg."

The attacks on Israel by Hamas on October 7th, 2023 have evidently complicated matters. In November, 2023, in the wake of the attacks, German Vice-Chancellor Robert Habeck issued an ominous warning that Muslims in Germany should "clearly distance themselves from antisemitism so as not to undermine their own right to tolerance."

I'm aware that I have tumbled down a slippery slope from books to state surveillance of people's activities. Book-banning arguments can be precarious that way. But let's retreat to the beginning of the German part of this story—to the banning of *Mein Kampf*. Taken by itself, does the postwar banning of *Mein Kampf* by the German government *incense* you? (I'm not asking whether you favor it.) I admit that it doesn't incense me.

IV

Which brings me to another question. The book-banning activities in the United States during these times have been well-documented elsewhere in this book. Attacks on libraries and librarians have gone fist-in-glove with curriculum-banning and other forms of intellectual and ideological suppression. Ellen Schrecker, a historian of the McCarthy era, described the attacks on American academic inquiry in 2021 as "worse than McCarthyism," and they have only worsened since that time.[9]

---

[9]Ellen Schrecker, "Yes, These Bills Are the New McCarthyism." *Academe Blog* September 12, 2021. https://academeblog.org/2021/09/12/yes-these-bills-are-the-new-mccarthyism/.

Yet and still: What if Florida's book-banning zealots were as energetically opposed to white supremacy as they are to diversity, African American Studies, or gender queerness?

What if they were to ban Thomas Dixon's noxious and reprehensible *Reconstruction Trilogy* of novels, whose popularity in the early twentieth century says a lot about the racialized character of American Progressivism? What if they were to ban D.W. Griffith's repulsive *Birth of a Nation*, a 1912 film based on one of those novels, *The Clansman* (1905), that quickly became the highest-grossing movie in American history, until that distinction was claimed by Walt Disney's 1933 *Snow White*? What if *Snow White* were banned? (She's not named Snow White for nothing, and as I write this, a live-action *Snow White* remake is being besieged by protests by disability activists as well as those concerned about race.)[10] If these infamous white supremacist entertainments were banned, I suspect that their only defenders on the left would be free speech absolutists like the American Civil Liberties Union (ACLU).

Law professor Stacy Hawkins recently argued that when the interests of academic freedom and Diversity, Equity, and Inclusion (DEI) collide, academic freedom should not automatically win. As she puts it:

If academic freedom is about protecting the robust exchange of ideas and the full engagement and participation of all members

---

[10]See Brooks Barnes, "Snow White and the Seven Kajillion Controversies." *The New York Times,* March 27, 2025. https://www.nytimes.com/2025/03/20/business/snow-white-movie-controversies.html.

of the academic community, it must account for the interests of both faculty and those students who are or feel marginalized.[11]

Maybe you agree with Hawkins or maybe you don't. I'm suggesting only that she's making a real argument that shouldn't be dismissed out of hand. At the same time, we should acknowledge that in practice, these sentiments have effectively banned any number of books from most college classrooms—including some in my own field of American literature. It's hard to find an American literature professor willing—let alone eager—to teach *Huckleberry Finn* these days. Not for nothing do book-banning and hate-speech measures often travel together.

These arguments over banning books pit classical liberalism (that is, freedom for the individual self) against communitarianism (acting for the good of the polity). The complication: Both liberalism and communitarianism are dear to both the political left and the political right in the United States. That's part of the reason that the current debates over book-banning are so vexing. I think that what we're seeing now—on each side of the spectrum, separately—is what happens when liberalism and communitarianism come into conflict within one system of thought: each side wants to ban its own set of books.

When it comes to officially banning books, the left privileges liberal ideals over communitarian ones—and so opposes the formal bans. But as I've just suggested, there are myriad academic settings these

---

[11]Stacy Hawkins, "Sometimes Diversity Trumps Academic Freedom." *The Chronicle of Higher Education* February 28, 2023. https://www.chronicle.com/article/sometimes-diversity-trumps-academic-freedom.

days where left-leaning communitarian values have been guiding campus policy, including curriculum, and these values have resulted in de facto bans of certain books.

For the US political right, the decision to ban books has communitarian motivations similar to the family-centered examples I began with: "we have to protect the children" above all. But when it comes to issues like campus speech, the right swings to the side of classical liberalism—they become free speech absolutists determined to protect the speech, and the books, that they hold dear.

Perhaps you agree with me that these contradictions are messy and not very coherent. (They do illustrate paradox.) But my point is that when it comes to banning books, saying "never" or "always" forecloses the sorts of complications that most people parse—not dismiss, but parse—every day. Such absolutism doesn't look closely. And why should it, when it doesn't have to?

In divided times, absolutist stances simply widen the distance between opposing points of view. One need not abandon one's beliefs to look closely at them—and also at those of one's opponents. Some negotiators have called for "interest-based bargaining," a kind of collaborative negotiation that begins with the different parties highlighting their own interests. The idea is to search for a solution that "maximizes common interests and reconciles conflicting ones."[12] If we are to find any possibility of shared interest in our troubled polity, we all might benefit from looking more closely at what the other people think.

---

[12]Fair Work Commission (Australia), "A Guide to Interest-Based Bargaining," August 12, 2024. https://www.fwc.gov.au/documents/resources/guide-interest-based-bargaining.pdf.

8

Reading *Howl* across the Iron Curtain, or Why Our Cold War Ideas About Banned Books May No Longer be Helping

Brian K. Goodman

If you're the kind of person who's worried about censorship in the United States today, you might know the black-and-white photograph of the poet-publisher Lawrence Ferlinghetti standing defiantly in front of a "Banned Books" display at his legendary City Lights Bookstore in San Francisco. The year is 1957. Under a handmade sign advertising "Banned Books," another proudly announces, "All books in window have been censored or suppressed at some point in the past." It's hard to make out all of the titles on display, but one pocket-sized City Lights edition hangs in the foreground: *Howl and Other Poems* by the Beat poet Allen Ginsberg, which had just been cleared of obscenity charges in a landmark trial that established new limits on the censorship of literature in the US.

The story of the *Howl* obscenity trial is also a story about the Cold War. On October 4, 1957, Judge Clayton W. Horn ruled that Ginsberg's poetry was not "without redeeming social importance," and therefore the sale of *Howl* could not be restricted.[1] The very next day the Soviet Union launched Sputnik into orbit, sparking a panic about America's disaffected youth. If the best minds of the postwar generation were really, in Ginsberg's words, "destroyed by madness, starving hysterical naked," then how would the US ever win the space race? A year later, in 1958, Herb Caen, a columnist at the *San Francisco Chronicle*, capitalized on this anxiety, coining the term "beatnik."

From the start, the story of the Beats was also entangled with the Cold War battle for freedom of expression. In his decision, Judge Horn asserted, "the best method of censorship is by the people as self-guardians of public opinion and not by government."[2] Much like the Cold War-era civil rights movement, the cause of free expression was both empowered and constrained by ideological rivalry with the Soviet Union. Not only did Cold War liberalism influence how the US legal system approached the issue of obscenity in literature, but anticommunism also shaped how American journalists covered the *Howl* trial in the news.

---

[1] Quoted in Bill Morgan, *Howl on Trial: The Battle for Free Expression* (San Francisco: City Lights Books, 2006), 197.
[2] Ibid., 198.

In a column titled "Iron Curtain on the Embarcadero," also published in the *Chronicle* in 1957, Abe Mellinkoff described how the entire *Howl* controversy began. That March, a customs officer named Chester McPhee ("a nice guy and a good public servant," who "knows no more about modern poetry than I do") had seized "520 copies of a book by an unknown poet named Allen Ginsberg."[3] Ginsberg's publisher, Ferlinghetti, had arranged for Ginsberg's debut poetry collection to be printed abroad in England, and then imported back into San Francisco. Prior to publication, Ferlinghetti also approached the ACLU for legal support. He was right to expect a scandal: according to the customs officer who seized the imported copies of *Howl*, "You wouldn't want your children to see it."[4] By the late fifties, however, this paternalistic justification for censoring literature was on its way to being replaced by a liberal conception of free expression that prized expertise over traditional sources of moral authority. As Mellinkoff closes his article in the *Chronicle*, "if a literary iron curtain is to be erected along the embarcadero, let's put some professors of literature down there to patrol it."[5]

Like most literature professors, I spend more time grading papers than I do patrolling the embarcadero. But as a specialist on Cold War literature, I also think a lot about censorship, both in the 1950s and today. Until recently, I was convinced that our contemporary debates about banned books in the US were still a product of the Cold War era. These days, as we continue to slide towards a novel form of

---

[3] Abe Mellinkoff, "Morning Report: Iron Curtain on the Embarcadero," *San Francisco Chronicle*, March 28, 1957.
[4] Ibid.
[5] Ibid.

authoritarianism in the US, I think we're in a new situation. If the Cold War still holds lessons for us today, we will need to pay more attention to the history of banned books across the Iron Curtain. And the lessons may not be what we expect.

***

The Cold War-era binary opposition between Soviet-bloc censorship and American free expression was always misleading. While I was researching my book about the circulation of so-called dissident literature across the Iron Curtain, I came across that iconic photograph of Ferlinghetti's "Banned Books" display in a surprising place: in a 1959 issue of a state-published journal of world literature from Soviet-aligned Czechoslovakia. The image of Ferlinghetti was reproduced in a feature article titled "American Bohemia" (*Americká bohéma*) that helped introduce Beat writing, including "Howl," to a Czech readership with only restricted access to contemporary US literature.[6] Like all other official publications in communist-era Czechoslovakia, the entire journal would have been subjected to pre-publication review by state censors at the Main Administration of Press Supervision (*Hlavní správa tiskového dohledu*), better known as the HSTD. To help get the first Czech translation of "Howl" past the censors, the editors of "American Bohemia" left out Ginsberg's playful reference to "Supercommunist pamphlets in Union Square."[7] But this small textual sacrifice served a larger cause.

---

[6] Igor Hájek, "Americká bohéma," *Světová literatura* 4, no. 6 (1959): 207–33.

[7] Here's the full line from "Howl" that was omitted: "who distributed Supercommunist pamphlets in Union Square weeping and undressing while the sirens of Los Alamos wailed them down, and wailed down Wall, and the Staten Island Ferry also wailed." See Allen Ginsberg, *Howl and Other Poems* (San Francisco: City Lights, 1956), 13.

"American Bohemia" hardly shies away from the topic of censorship. The entire discussion of the Beat phenomenon is introduced by an account of the *Howl* obscenity trial. "The public prosecutor requested that the slim booklet be declared an immoral and youth-corrupting pamphlet, so that its sale would be prohibited," the author, Igor Hájek, explains to his Czech readers, who were quite familiar with the puritanism of Communist Party hardliners in their own country.[8] Given their recent experience of Stalinism, then, how did this discussion of suppressed literature make it past the censors?

The cynical explanation is obvious enough: the *Howl* trial presented a perfect opportunity to point out US hypocrisy on the topic of cultural freedom. Not only was Ginsberg raised in a Jewish left-wing milieu, but he was an outspoken critic of the conformism of US political culture during the early Cold War years. Even though *Howl*'s publishers were exonerated, the initial seizure and prosecution was a reminder that, yes, in fact, literary censorship did also exist in the US. To underscore this point, Hájek makes several references to the stifling atmosphere of *mccarthyismus*, or McCarthyism, that constrained free expression across US media and higher education in the early Cold War years.

But "American Bohemia" was not a work of Cold War propaganda. Rather, it was an attempt by a small group of liberal editors, critics, and translators to help open up Czech literary culture after the end of Stalinism. In the years after the Soviet leader Nikita Khrushchev had denounced Stalin's cult of personality in 1956, political reform in Czechoslovakia had been slow to arrive. Literature, including foreign translations, became a second front in the battle over cultural

---

[8] Hájek, "Americká bohéma," 207.

de-Stalinization. The issue of censorship played a central role in debates over the future of state socialism across the entire Eastern bloc.

Just as book bans have always existed in the United States, the political control of imaginative literature in the communist world was never total. Even during the Stalinist era, there were cracks in the system. During the Thaw of the late fifties and sixties, some of those cracks were pried open. Through a complex set of negotiations, a new generation of writers, editors, translators, and even censors could find ways to get nonconformist writing, including American Beat literature, into the hands of readers.

Thanks in part to the opening of Eastern bloc archives after the end of the Cold War, we now know a lot about how literary censorship operates across different types of political regimes, from the Enlightenment era up until today. Instead of dividing the world between freedom and totalitarianism, we can learn much more by comparing specific features of paternalistic, liberal, and authoritarian regimes of censorship across different historical periods.[9] According to the paternalistic model that predominated in parts of eighteenth-century Europe, religious and political authorities were required to approve all texts *before* publication. In liberal censorship regimes, as in the Cold War-era US, the publication of all texts is permitted, at least in theory, until they are explicitly banned. Legal decisions about what kinds of texts are prohibited or allowed are open to public

---

[9]If like me, you always fantasized about reading a two-volume, 1,600-page history of censorship in the Czech lands, check out *V obecném zájmu: Cenzura a sociální regulace literatury v moderní české kultuře, 1749–2014* (Prague: Academia, 2015), edited by Michael Wögerbauer, Petr Píša, Petr Šámal, Pavel Janáček, et. al. Covering all the periods mentioned above, the title in English translates to *In the Public Interest Censorship and the Social Regulation of Literature in Modern Czech Culture, 1749–2014.*

scrutiny and debate. Think of the *Howl* trial. We might understand the authoritarian model as a reaction against this liberal conception of censorship. Authoritarian regimes utilize a dispersed system of both pre- and post-publication censorship to promote a specific cultural or political project. In authoritarian societies, decisions about censorship are usually hidden from public view.

But there are also some commonalities across different regime types. For instance, censors rarely conceive of their work as only punitive. By comparing state censorship practices in eighteenth-century France, the nineteenth-century British Raj, and twentieth-century East Germany, the cultural historian Robert Darnton has shown how censors in all three regimes actually viewed their role in positive terms.[10] In communist societies, including in Czechoslovakia, most censors believed they were contributing to projects of mass literacy and education while helping to build a new socialist literature.

What does that mean for us today? Perhaps we should imagine our own twenty-first century censors in cardigans and reading glasses rather than in red hats and jackboots. To be sure, there are now authoritarian government officials and other petty tyrants in our communities seeking to censor what we read, but we should also understand that many of the parents challenging books at local libraries genuinely believe they are on the side of literary education. Even in supposedly liberal societies like the US, the line between

---

[10]See Robert Darnton, *Censors at Work: How States Shaped Literature* (New York: Norton, 2014). Relatedly, the Czech scholar Petr Šámal, a leading scholar of communist-era censorship in Czechoslovakia, translates the HSTD's full name as "the Central Office of the Guardians of the Printed Word," which, however Orwellian, does convey how many HSTD censors conceived of their own work.

rightwing authoritarianism and everyday paternalism is not always so easy to draw.

The good news, if there is any, is that total control of literature has always been an illusion. The consequences of book bans are unpredictable. On both sides of the Iron Curtain, book bans have often had the paradoxical effect of attracting even more attention to a proscribed text. The *Howl* trial is, once again, a great example. Hájek, the author of "American Bohemia," understood this dynamic well. According to Hájek, "the most interesting feature of the [*Howl*] trial—of which there are many held annually in the United States— was that it was the first time the public learned about the existence of a new literary movement."[11] As Hájek knew firsthand, this was also true of banned literature in Thaw-era Czechoslovakia. The book historian Jiřina Šmejkalová has pointed out, "the stamp of 'previously forbidden text' was perhaps the best advertising to attract an audience to a book."[12]

Again and again, scholars have shown that censorship does not only perform a restrictive function. It can also be generative in ways a regime doesn't expect. In Eastern bloc societies, authoritarian censorship helped produce dynamic underground literary scenes, including unofficial publishing and distribution networks that circulated banned literature in samizdat form. The line dividing

---

[11]Hájek, "Americká bohéma," 207.

[12]Jiřina Šmejkalová, "Censoring Canons: Transitions and Prospects of Literary Institutions in Czechoslovakia," in *The Administration of Aesthetic: Censorship, Political Criticism and the Public Sphere*, ed. Richard Burt (Minneapolis: Minnesota University Press, 1994), 201. See also Šmejkalová, *Cold War Books in the "Other" Europe and What Came After* (Boston: Brill, 2011); Roar Lishaugen and Šmejkalová, "Reading East of the Berlin Wall," *PMLA* 134, no. 1 (January 2019): 178–87.

unofficial and official culture was porous. In Prague, a small but thriving Beat subculture existed in the early sixties, fed in part by the official translations introduced by essays like "American Bohemia."

Banned writers sometimes become a source of surprising cultural authority. When Allen Ginsberg traveled across the Iron Curtain to visit Prague in person in 1965, he was already well known to members of the city's youth counterculture. During a massive student demonstration, Ginsberg was elected the ceremonial "King of May" and then kicked out of the country by the Czechoslovak political authorities. As I describe in my book, Ginsberg's visit and expulsion were an important milestone on the road to the Prague Spring.[13] In 1968, Czechoslovak reformers, including members of the literary intelligentsia like Hájek, attempted a rare synthesis between liberalism and socialism, prioritizing the abolition of state censorship. If successful, this experiment might have destabilized the entire Cold War balance of power. In August of 1968, however, Soviet tanks rolled into Prague, putting an end to the short-lived experiment of "socialism with a human face." As Ginsberg wrote in a poem inspired by his misadventures in Prague, "May was too beautiful to last for more than a month."[14]

✳✳✳

Twenty years after the Prague Spring, Ginsberg's "Howl" was back in the US news. In 1988, the Federal Communications Commission (FCC) attempted to ban broadcasts of obscene material until after

---

[13]See Brian Goodman, *The Nonconformists: American and Czech Writers across the Iron Curtain* (Cambridge: Harvard UP, 2023).
[14]See Ginsberg, "Kral Majales," in *Planet News, 1961–1967* (San Francisco: City Lights Books, 1968), 91.

midnight, leading one radio network to remove a reading of "Howl" from a scheduled program on (ironically enough) censorship.[15] In a radio interview titled "Why He Can't Broadcast 'Howl,'" Ginsberg tried to make the FCC's new policy into a public scandal by—once again—invoking Cold War politics.[16] "It's very similar to what goes on in the Soviet censorship bureaucracy," he told the interviewer. "But I think it's the last desperate gasp of the Reagan neo-conservatives."[17]

Ginsberg was far too optimistic. Rather than ushering in a golden age of free expression, the end of the Cold War brought with it a new wave of rightwing cultural regulation in the United States. Writing in 1994, the censorship scholar Richard Burt provided a partial list of conservative attempts to purge moral obscenity from the American arts: "Attacks on publicly funded exhibitions of artists like Robert Mapplethorpe and Andres Serrano, on MTV videos, on rap music by 2-Live Crew and Ice-T, and on television advertisements as well as the FBI's seizure of works and equipment of photographers like Jock Sturges on the grounds that they are child pornographers."[18]

---

[15]"Howl" was an obvious target. A year earlier, the FCC had threatened to penalize radio stations that broadcast "material that depicts or describes, in terms patently offensive as measured by contemporary community standards for the broadcast medium, sexual or excretory activities or organs." See Andrew L. Yarrow, "Allen Ginsberg's 'Howl' in a New Controversy," *New York Times*, January 6, 1968. https://www.nytimes.com/1988/01/06/arts/allen-ginsberg-s-howl-in-a-new-controversy.html.

[16]Since 1965, Ginsberg had remained active in the battle for freedom of expression, including becoming a member of PEN's Freedom-to-Write committee. The same year as the FCC controversy, in 1988, "he compiled a document highlighting the censorship activities of the Israeli authorities in Palestine which the committee used in a letter of protest against Israel's actions in the occupied territories." See Ian D. Copestake, "Allen Ginsberg," in *Censorship: A World Encyclopedia* (London: Fitzroy Dearborn, 2001), 956.

[17]Quoted in Yarrow, "Allen Ginsberg's 'Howl' in a New Controversy" https://www.nytimes.com/1988/01/06/arts/allen-ginsberg-s-howl-in-a-new-controversy.html.

[18]Richard Burt, "Introduction: The 'New' Censorship," in *Administration of Aesthetics*, xi.

The culture wars of the nineties brought Cold War discourses about communist censorship back to the home front. With the support of many free speech liberals, neoconservative intellectuals and politicians were able to weaponize free expression in order to attack internal enemies on the US left. "Political correctness," an ironic term of self-critique that originated among left-wing activists, was a weak substitute for the institutional forms of censorship recently associated with the Soviet Union.

In the nineties, everyone was against censorship, and yet censorship was supposedly everywhere. Burt influentially referred to this paradoxical situation as "the new censorship." Drawing on the theories of thinkers like Michel Foucault and Pierre Bourdieu, scholars of the new censorship argued that some degree of cultural regulation—whether carried out by state institutions, the capitalist marketplace, or informal social pressure—is not only inevitable but constitutive of all literary communication. This led to some definitional confusion. As Burt put it, "standing against censorship, whether it is practiced by the left or by the right, depends on a list of censors so heterogeneous that the term *censorship* becomes meaningless."[19] A corollary view about the meaninglessness of freedom of expression was most famously articulated by Stanley Fish in his 1994 essay, "There's No Such Thing as Free Speech, And It's a Good Thing, Too." If censorship was everywhere, free expression was suddenly nowhere to be found.

Reading banned books across the Iron Curtain can help us cut through some of this confusion. Following the lead of scholars of censorship in the former Eastern bloc, we should distinguish between

---

[19]Richard Burt, "Introduction: The 'New' Censorship," in *Administration of Aesthetics*, xxv.

institutional forms of censorship and weaker sources of cultural regulation, including political correctness (or what the right now calls "woke ideology"). As the German scholar Beate Müller puts it, "one could criticize such a wider view of censorship as misleading because it runs the risk of equating very different forms of control by confusing censorship with social norms affecting and controlling communication."[20] In 1988, Ginsberg referred to the wider "chilling effect" of state regulation of speech, whether on the radio or in print.[21] Self-censorship, one form of anticipatory obedience, is a real problem. But what distinguishes self-censorship from other forms of voluntary social discretion is the existence of institutional forms of censorship or the threat of official sanction. A big reason I have moved towards a stricter definition of censorship in my own work is because I've seen how Cold War-era discourses about self-censorship were appropriated during the culture wars of the nineties.

Here, I think, lie the seeds of our own era. But today, there is one very important difference: since the end of the Cold War, freedom of expression has lost the ideological warrant once provided by the geopolitical rivalry with the Soviet Union, and its authoritarian model of state censorship.[22] In the US, the phrase "free speech" is now a floating signifier in a rightwing war of position being waged against the left-liberal intelligentsia. The resulting situation is not great.

---

[20]Beate Müller, "Censorship and Cultural Regulation: Mapping the Territory," in *Censorship and Cultural Regulation in the Modern Age* (Amsterdam; New York: Rodopi, 2004), 9.

[21]Quoted in Yarrow, "Allen Ginsberg's 'Howl' in a New Controversy," https://www.nytimes.com/1988/01/06/arts/allen-ginsberg-s-howl-in-a-new-controversy.html.

[22]To my mind, this has had a much bigger effect on contemporary free speech discourse than the rise of deconstruction in literature departments. Here, I wonder if the arguments of deconstructionists like Stanley Fish were symptoms rather than causes.

Everyone is now a free speech cynic; meanwhile, the book bans are back, and the Cold War atmosphere of *mccarthyismus* has returned. Meanwhile, collusion between authoritarian state actors, cultural conservatives, the tech oligarchy, and a consolidated corporate media are producing novel forms of institutional censorship that we still don't fully understand or know how to name.

So, what is to be done? Beat writers like Ginsberg believed literary free expression was an end in itself. But to reinvigorate liberal protections against state censorship, we will need more than just poetry. We may need our own Prague Spring. This new movement in support of an integrated approach to free expression that also prioritizes social and economic equality will take years to build. Call it free speech liberalism with a human face. In the meantime, we should learn from Cold War history on both sides of the Iron Curtain and put the banned books back on display.

9
Banning the Enlightenment

Aaron Santesso

In the latest horrible news, book bans are coming back into fashion—a Cold War relic, now *de rigueur* for any conservative activist (and/or presidential hopeful). The overwhelming majority of books singled out for cleansing are recently published works that focus on LGBTQ themes or race. But a handful of classics still make the cut to be cut, as it were: from Kurt Vonnegut in Gladwin, MI and James Baldwin in Clay County, FL all the way back to Chaucer in Wentzville, MO. Nottaway County, Virginia's list of "sexually explicit" books to be avoided includes *Twelfth Night*, *Macbeth*, *Beowulf*, and *The Importance of Being Earnest*.

Academics and op-ed columnists have been wringing their hands over what this means for America's youth. I have my own, entirely selfish concerns. After looking through a masochistically large number of these lists, I can report that I have not encountered a single work from the eighteenth century. As someone who teaches eighteenth-century literature, I know I should be happy about this. But on some level, it feels like a slight. Are there really no eighteenth-century texts as edgy or boundary-pushing or "sexually explicit" as *Beowulf*? Jonathan Swift's *Gulliver's Travels* features attempted rape, public urination, plus a detailed description of pubic hair. Daniel Defoe's *Moll Flanders* could hardly contain more bannable material. Likewise for Henry Fielding's *Tom Jones* and Samuel Richardson's *Clarissa*. Yet none of these eighteenth-century texts get a mention. What do you have to do to get cancelled in this town?

One reason to be nervous about this is that the period's absence from conservative ban lists seems to align somewhat uncomfortably with the pop-academic idea that eighteenth-century texts and ideas are naturally right-wing friendly. A number of progressive writers have been pushing such claims recently. One laments "the present-day impact of ideals forged in the 1600s and 1700s" (to wit: the Kyle Rittenhouse verdict was "due to America's Founding Fathers embracing Locke's absurd ideas"); another suggests that the "legacy" of the eighteenth century is "Enlightenment ideas of race and white supremacy."

Serious academics have long issued more nuanced versions of this argument. Roger Eatwell argued that "fascism is … a product of the Enlightenment"; Stanley Payne suggested that "[a]ll of Hitler's political ideas had their origin in the Enlightenment"; Isaiah Berlin concluded that "Hitler and Mussolini [were Rousseau's] heirs." And of course, Adorno and Horkheimer famously argued that the oppression underlying right-wing authoritarianism is built on Enlightenment values: the suppression of nature and emotion in favor of rationality leads to a world built around prediction and control.

A parallel position has been floating around among modern far-right thinkers. Remember the "Dark Enlightenment"? It was a real concern a few years ago. At a time when a number of our political leaders began openly questioning democracy, here was a movement arguing that authoritarian rule was the way forward—and finding support for this position in eighteenth-century thought. This wasn't just another sad alt-right subset; it seemed to have real reach and influence. Steve Bannon was a fan. Tucker Carlson talked about it on his show. Various eighteenth-century ideas and texts started to circulate in worrying ways. Curtis Yarvin, the de-facto intellectual leader of the school, described himself as a "Jacobite." Over at Breitbart, columnists discussed Edmund Burke and quoted Edward Gibbon's *The Decline and Fall of the Roman Empire* as justifications for Trumpian anti-immigration policies.

For a moment, it felt possible that the eighteenth century might go the way of medieval studies: a newly notorious academic field linked in the popular mind with neo-Nazi thought. It didn't happen, of course: for the moment, eighteenth-century studies remains a safely obscure area of academic activity—the kind of field that elicits polite, slightly confused nods and awkward pauses when people ask what you do. Nevertheless, one continues to encounter a weirdly unshakeable belief in the essential, inherent conservatism of eighteenth-century thought—in the idea of the "EnRightenment," to use an unfortunate term that I overheard at a conference and have been trying to forget ever since.

It's one thing, however, to suggest that the eighteenth century is friendly ground for anti-progressives, and another to suggest that anti-progressives actually have any real interest in the period—that the absence of the eighteenth century from book ban and challenge lists is *intentional*. Happily (I use the word loosely), there are ways to measure actual right-wing enthusiasm for eighteenth-century texts. Consider, for example, the surge of "approved books" lists, issued both by (mainly Republican) state education boards and (mainly conservative) NGOs. Do eighteenth-century books make it on to these lists at statistically significant rates?

We might begin with the one that has received the most media attention: Florida's "Stop WOKE Act"-inspired "approved books" list, with its 350 scrupulously DEI and progressivism-free titles. Here is the complete list of eighteenth-century literary works approved for grades 10–12: the "Poetry of Robert Burns" and something called "The Chimney Sweepers poems from Songs of Innocence." There are no eighteenth-century novels, plays, or satires (Swift's "Modest Proposal" is included in the approved books for the "Nineth [sic] Grade").

There are, however, several works of political philosophy on the 10th–12th grade list: Locke's *Two Treatises of Government*; Rousseau's *On the Social Contract*; *The Spirit of the Laws* by Montesquieu; "Doctrine of Right," from Immanuel Kant's *Metaphysics of Morals*; Paine's *Common Sense*; *The Federalist Papers*, George Washington's "Farewell Address," and *Sinners in the Hands* by Jonathan Edwards. Not much of a list—but even this small selection does indeed represent an unusually robust crop of Enlightenment works, relatively speaking. Normally, in such official reading lists, the eighteenth century is invisible.

A number of states focus entirely on modern works (the books on California's recommended list date all the way back to the late

Obama era), but even those states that include older texts generally steer clear of the eighteenth century. New York's list includes a total of zero works of fiction published in the 1700s (Jane Austen's *Pride and Prejudice* is as close as we get), and one work of poetry: William Blake's "Tiger, Tiger" (not actually the title of the work, by the way, but let's go ahead and count it). The Jordan School District in Utah features *Gulliver's Travels* along with Voltaire's *Candide* and two works by Oliver Goldsmith: *She Stoops to Conquer* and *Vicar of Wakefield*—but that's out of a list of 512 works.

So, do conservative state education boards, school districts, and parents' groups recommend eighteenth-century works at a higher rate than progressive, liberal, and centrist lists? In terms of political and philosophical texts, perhaps (although not strikingly so). But conservative reading lists, on the whole, rarely include literary works from the period.

The Mississippi Department of Education's recommended books list for grades 9–12, which includes works by Ovid, Chaucer, Shakespeare, and numerous other pre-modern authors, mentions only the *Autobiography of Benjamin Franklin* and *Candide* (*Frankenstein* is a near-miss). The Texas Education Agency? It recommends *King Lear* and *Pride and Prejudice*, but avoids the eighteenth century entirely. The Arkansas Education Alliance's list of works that home-schooled students should "have some level of familiarity with" has one eighteenth-century literary work: Defoe's *Robinson Crusoe* (not in their main list, but in the second-tier "Other Notable Books"). Focus on the Family's list of recommended books for teens includes no eighteenth-century works (adjacent periods are represented by John Bunyan's *Pilgrim's Progress* and Sir Walter Scott's *Ivanhoe*). The

Young America Foundation includes *The Federalist Papers* and the Constitution, but no eighteenth-century literature at all (they do find space for two novels by George Orwell ... and twelve by Brad Thor).

So much for mainstream conservative groups. What about the actual, self-proclaimed "heirs to Hitler and Mussolini"? Are members of the far right any more enthusiastic about eighteenth-century books than moderate conservatives? Again, we can turn to reading lists (and yes, such lists do exist; there are book clubs for the polos-and-khakhis set). The kind of eighteenth-century texts recommended by the far right tend, again, to be works of political science. The "Free Man's Reading List" includes John Locke's *Second Treatise*, Adam Smith, and Edmund Burke (as well as Thomas Paine and Immanuel Kant). No literature, though.

Neo-reactionary reading lists include very few eighteenth-century literary authors. The r/neoreactionary subreddit's list of books to be familiar with mentions Burke, again, plus Joseph de Maistre, but no literature. The kids over at 4chan's /lit/ board? Their Top 100 Books of All Time includes only one eighteenth-century work (Laurence Sterne's *Tristram Shandy*, from out of nowhere). Milo Yannopoulous's and Michelle Malkin's extensive "America First Reading List"? Only *Robinson Crusoe* ("one man's struggle to find his faith"), along with Swift's "Modest Proposal" and *Gulliver's Travels* ("a novel satirizing various aspects of human culture") make the cut. Again, there is a level of interest in eighteenth-century *thought* in their list (Burke, Smith, and Alexis de Tocqueville are on there), but in terms of literature, not much makes it. Douglas Murray, writing in the *Spectator*, claims that a UK government ministry had a few years ago composed a "red-flag" list of literature that indicated a movement toward right-wing radicalization, and that this list included Thomas Hobbes' *Leviathan*, Locke's *Two Treatises of Government*, Burke's *Reflection on the Revolution in France*, and select works by Smith. No literary works were mentioned.

Given the polite level of respect for eighteenth-century conservative *thinkers* on these lists, why aren't more eighteenth-century literary authors featured? Are they not "Stop WOKE"-ish enough? Well, no. It's not as though the period's literature lacks for anti-progressive options: anti-democratic and authoritarian writing, xenophobic works, homophobic works—it's all there. There are plenty of isolationist, nativist poems, for example, from John Gilbert Cooper's England-First style "The Genius of Britain" ("Learn, Britons, hence you want no foreign friends, / the Lion's safety on himself depends") to Charles Churchill's "The Times," which argues that homosexuality, brought in mainly from "the soft luxurious EAST" via Italy ("nurse of ev'ry softer art"), has ruined the native English manliness that once upheld the nation. There are poems complaining about the lawless poor avoiding taxes while the decent, wealthy sort have to pay them (Mary Alcock's "Instructions, Supposed to Be Written in Paris, for a Mob in England" is a treasure trove of this sort of sentiment). There are Islamophobic works a-plenty. Conservatives of the more extreme type are spoiled for reading choices, really.

And, of course, even more mainstream eighteenth-century works could be made to fit an alt-right agenda, if a reader is determined enough. The "America First Reading List" includes Mark Twain's *Huck Finn* and James Joyce's *Portrait of the Artist* ("a novel about … spiritual awakening"), after all. Were you aware, for example, that Jane Austen has become a favorite author for white supremacists? Compared to

Pride and Prejudice, Samuel Johnson's *Rasselas*—a work that features a nation safely ensconced behind an impermeable border wall, watched at all times by "sentinels," that only opens its gate once a year, holding auditions for a small number of talented new immigrants—feels like a natural pick for a certain type of reading list. But nary a mention of it anywhere.

The question remains: why is the alt-right not recommending *more* eighteenth-century literature? One answer that has been gleefully forwarded innumerable times over the past few years is the "scientific" claim that literature is naturally unappealing to conservatives because it is too deeply connected to empathy, and empathy is an inherently progressive emotion. Now, those of us who teach literature for a living understand the appeal of this argument. We rarely push back too hard against the highly dubious assertion that conservatives (who adopt children and donate to charity at higher rates) are measurably less empathetic than progressives. It's certainly pleasant to think that the literature business is driven by empathy, and that anyone teaching literature is automatically a player in the empathy game. But let's face facts here: more than a million copies of Ayn Rand's novels are sold in an average year, and they are among the least empathetic documents ever fashioned by human hand. Also: there are brilliant authors and literary critics out there who aren't exactly renowned for their empathy. And however we look at it, we still run up against the fact that there are vast numbers of conservative readers of literature of all sorts. Shakespeare gets plenty of conservative love, and he's as empathetic an author as our species has produced, surely.

So again: why so little eighteenth-century literature? A mid-1990s Modern Language Association poll, taken at the height of the Culture Wars (first wave), asked members of the general public what they thought about English professors. Finally, MLA members were promised, we would get some answers. Did the average person think of English professors as anti-American communists, or as well-meaning but ineffectual nerds? The results were clear: the average person didn't think about English professors at all.

Something similar is plainly going on with eighteenth-century literature. People simply don't think about it much anymore. In an age of disappearing English majors and a defunct canon, eighteenth-century literature no longer possesses enough cultural capital to justify its presence on politically-minded reading lists. Political and philosophical texts from the period arguably continue to hold on to some vestiges of prestige: Burke and Kant are still names to conjure with, for a fringe-right movement looking for historical and cultural legitimization. This is not to say that the alt-right are actually reading Burke and Kant, any more than would-be medievalist neo-nazis are reading Julian of Norwich and the Venerable Bede (if they're reading anyone, they're reading Tolkien and other purveyors of cosplay medievalism). But at least there is some capital in the names and reputations of "Burke" and "Kant." What capital do Pope and Gray and Richardson still possess? None. It's like William Beckford is *trying* to get banned in *Vathek*. But who now reads *Vathek*?

Years ago, I attended a symposium of artists and scholars working on surveillance. Everyone talked about the fear of finding out you were under surveillance. A Chinese artist explained that for him, and for most artists he knew at home, the real fear was finding out that you were *not* the target of surveillance. It meant you didn't matter. It meant no one was worried about your work. The fact that eighteenth-century books are not being targeted by the book-banners is not encouraging. It means we're not worth the energy to cancel. We can't even get into the game to be thrown out of it.

I don't have the space here to explore the larger question of *why* the literature of the period has lost its cultural capital. (It certainly doesn't help that many of the great prose works it produced are thousand-page picaresque and epistolary novels that don't necessarily lend themselves to modern, bingeable adaptations.) In any case, we needn't lose hope. It's not beyond our power to change this situation. These book challenges don't emanate from a scattering of random readers around the country. They are usually highly coordinated, if not outright Astro-turfed; a Facebook group or the like identifies a thematically-troubling book; the offending title becomes the focus of strategy sessions; not long after, Toni Morrison's *The Bluest Eye* is challenged in multiple Utah counties simultaneously (this happened).

If we can raise the profile of one or two eighteenth-century books, we might be able to gain this kind of traction, and finally get the eighteenth century back into the public conversation. I'd like to suggest Tobias Smollett's *Roderick Random* as a test case. It has gay characters. It contains anti-military and anti-church themes. It has anti-racist language (admittedly a stretch: Random describes his experience in slave trading as "disagreeable," but we can sell it). If just one person decides that these themes are objectionable, *Roderick Random* might find its way onto an offensive book list, at which point it will almost certainly be officially challenged and at least temporarily banned, possibly across dozens of school districts. Suddenly, a work of eighteenth-century literature will have made it into the game. It will, technically speaking, be relevant to modern American life and political discourse. And why stop there? We can get *Moll Flanders* onto these lists! We can get people up in arms about Richardson's *Pamela*!

And if we work hard enough, we can have people from coast to coast worried about the spectre of Enlightenment values, and about the idea of our children encountering works written in the spirit of egalitarianism, toleration, and liberal reason.

10
Why It's Okay to Call It a Ban

Emily Harris

Annie's Foundation was born in Johnston, Iowa, in the fall of 2021—when six moms who had never planned on becoming activists found themselves at school board meetings, standing up for their kids' right to read.

The spark? A book challenge led by a Moms for Liberty member—someone who didn't even have a child in the district—who demanded the removal of *The Hate U Give* and *The Absolutely True Diary of a Part-Time Indian* from a 10th grade classroom. That parent didn't just want to control what her own kids could read–she wanted to make that decision for everyone else's children, too.

Among those who spoke out was Ann, a fierce mother of three whose advocacy had become a regular force at school board meetings. When Ann passed away unexpectedly in 2022, we created Annie's Foundation to carry on her spirit of advocacy and her unwavering belief in the power of stories.

Annie's Foundation is a grassroots organization that works to protect students' right to read, advocate for diverse and inclusive education, and fight censorship in Iowa public schools. We show up at board meetings, file public records requests, support students and educators, create access to banned and challenged titles through book giveaways, and expose the political machinery behind coordinated book bans.

Today, the fight against censorship is intensifying—but so is our determination.

As we began organizing, showing up at meetings, and sharing what we were seeing, we kept hearing the same deflection from book ban supporters—an attempt to minimize, distort, and distract from what was really happening: "Nobody is actually banning books."

The Word They Hate

Proponents of book bans work hard to control the narrative. They insist a book isn't truly banned unless it's no longer published or available anywhere. If you can still find it at a bookstore or a public library, they argue, it doesn't count.

Let's be clear: That's not how banning works.

They reject the term "book ban" for a reason—because history is not kind to book banners. From slaveholders to Nazis, those who suppress ideas and silence voices are never remembered as the heroes. And deep down, they know it.

Before the Civil War, books describing the horrors of slavery—like *Uncle Tom's Cabin*—were routinely censored in the South. Enslaved people were even denied access to the Bible, out of fear they'd discover the story of Moses leading his people to freedom.

The Nazis burned thousands of books written by Jewish authors, political dissidents, and intellectuals who challenged their ideology. Works by Albert Einstein, Sigmund Freud, Helen Keller, Ernest Hemingway, and others were tossed into the flames.

It probably doesn't feel great to be associated with Nazis or slave owners, which is why modern-day book banners work so hard to disguise what they're doing. But make no mistake; today's book bans follow the same playbook: restrict access to ideas you don't like, then insist it's for the public good.

And they're not just rebranding censorship—they're legislating it. Passed in 2023 under pressure from far-right groups like Moms for Liberty, Iowa's SF496 requires public schools to remove any book that contains a "description or depiction of a sex act," regardless of how brief or educationally relevant the content may be. As a result, books like *Slaughterhouse-Five*, *Brave New World*, *Beloved*, *The Bluest Eye*, *1984*, and *The Handmaid's Tale* have been pulled—not because they're harmful, but because they challenge traditional narratives about race, gender, trauma, and identity.

So ... What Is a Book Ban, Really?

A ban, simply put, is when something is officially or legally prohibited. When a book is removed from a public-school library or classroom because of its content, it has been banned—regardless of whether it's still available for purchase elsewhere.

Once a book is included in a public school library, students have a First Amendment right to access it. Removing it for ideological or political reasons is censorship—and it's unconstitutional.

Book banners try to sidetrack the conversation by insisting kids can "just get it somewhere else." But that argument is both elitist and legally irrelevant.

Not every family can afford to buy books. Not every student has access to a public library, transportation to get there, or even the knowledge of which book they're looking for. Telling a student to "just find it elsewhere" doesn't solve the problem. It simply shifts responsibility away from schools and onto families, many of whom are already under-resourced.

It's also logically incoherent. If book banners truly believe these books are so dangerous that they must be removed from school libraries, how does it make sense to suggest that kids go read them somewhere else? In Iowa, supporters of SF496 claim the law is necessary to protect children from "pornographic" or "obscene" material in schools. Under this law, any book containing a depiction or description of a sex act must be removed—no matter the context, and regardless of its literary, historical, or educational value.

As a result, schools have pulled a wide variety of books: classics like *I Know Why the Caged Bird Sings*, *As I Lay Dying*, and *The Color Purple*; award-winning works by Toni Morrison, John Green, and Jodi Picoult; nonfiction titles; books that appear on AP exams; and even those intended to help students understand or recover from sexual violence.

If these books are truly "pornographic," as lawmakers claim, it defies logic to suggest children can simply access them at public libraries or bookstores. Providing pornographic material to minors is illegal in any setting—whether it's in schools, libraries, or retail stores.

The contradiction is clear: book banners argue that a book is too obscene for a school library, yet simultaneously imply it's perfectly acceptable for a child to access it elsewhere. It's as if books have chameleon-like properties—pornographic in schools, but harmless in bookstores. That argument isn't just irrational, it reveals the fundamental dishonesty of the campaign.

And the hypocrisy doesn't end there. These groups are now actively working to remove the same books from public libraries and to pressure bookstores to stop selling them. The message is unmistakable: this was never just about schools. It was never about parental choice. The goal is erasure.

And as courts—including the US Supreme Court—have consistently ruled, the government cannot justify infringing on someone's rights by arguing those rights could be exercised somewhere else.

In *Southeastern Promotions v. Conrad* (1975), the Court held that a city could not block a theater performance of *Hair*, even if other venues were available. The First Amendment doesn't come with fine print. It protects access in public spaces, including public schools.

That same principle applied in *Case v. Unified School District No. 233* (1995), when a Kansas school board removed *Annie on My Mind*, a novel about two teenage girls in love. The board argued students could still access the book elsewhere. The court rejected that claim outright. Removing it from the library was unconstitutional.

In Iowa, a federal judge recently enjoined the enforcement of SF496, finding it unconstitutional, and flat-out rejected the idea that it's okay to strip books from school libraries just because students might find them somewhere else.

What We've Learned—and What You Can Do

Book banners want us distracted by definitions. They want us arguing over semantics instead of noticing that kids are losing access to books they need. But here's what we've learned: you don't have to be an expert to push back. You just have to care enough to act.

That's how Annie's Foundation started. We weren't policy pros. We were parents who saw something wrong in our schools and refused to stay quiet. We showed up, we spoke out, and we organized.

Since then, we've spoken at school board meetings, filed ethics complaints, and supported students who've testified in front of lawmakers. We've tracked book bans, challenged policies, and called out the politicians and groups fueling this movement. Every single book we hand out carries a sticker with Ann's name on it—a reminder that one person's courage can spark a movement. As of September 2025, we've put more than 18,000 diverse books into the hands of Iowa students and families.

We've also used public records requests to expose what's happening in our schools. One district quietly removed more than 300 books from its shelves, even banning a children's cookbook just because it showed a teddy bear in a rainbow sweater. No public notice. No vote. Just erasure.

By demanding transparency district by district, we're building a record of what's being banned and why. That data matters—not just for fighting censorship now, but for documenting its impact and holding those responsible accountable.

And we've seen others rise up, too:

- In 2023, Iowa voters rejected 12 out of 13 school board candidates who ran on a Moms for Liberty platform.
- Students across the state have organized banned book clubs and spoken directly to lawmakers about the impact of censorship.
- Libraries and bookstores have launched displays, reading challenges, and public events that proudly celebrate the very books being targeted.
- Banned books sales have increased in the last few years, indicating the people are willing to put their money where harm is being done.

You can take action in your own community too:

- Start a watchdog group like Annie's Foundation—even if it begins with just a few parents paying attention. That's how we started, too.
- Use public records requests to uncover what's really happening in your schools. Shine a light on soft censorship and behind-the-scenes decisions.
- Hold journalists accountable. Demand that they stop treating book banners as good-faith actors and start reporting on them as the well-funded, politically connected astroturf groups they are.
- Push your school district to adopt clear, transparent policies for how books are reviewed and selected—and insist that they stand firm when the pressure comes.

- Support students as they lead the fight for inclusive education and access to stories that reflect their lived experiences.
- Call on lawmakers and courts to protect the First Amendment and reject efforts to legislate fear, bias, and control.

Book bans thrive on silence, shame, and misinformation. But when communities respond with truth, transparency, and relentless love for kids and books alike, censorship loses its grip.

So if you're reading this and wondering where to start, start here: Show up. Speak up. Pass the book. File the records request. Call the media. Ask who's behind the curtain—and why.

And yes, in case you're wondering—they banned *The Wizard of Oz*, too. In 1986, a group of fundamentalist Christian families in Greeneville, Tennessee, tried to remove *The Wonderful Wizard of Oz* from the public-school curriculum. Their objections? The book supposedly promoted occultism, secular humanism, evolution, disobedience to parents, pacifism, and feminism. They especially objected to the idea of "good witches," arguing it was theologically impossible, citing the Bible's directive: "thou shalt not suffer a witch to live." A federal judge ruled that their children could opt out of the lessons, but the families were unsatisfied; they wanted it banned for all children.

Representing them in court was Michael Farris, a lawyer who would go on to become one of the key architects of the modern parental rights movement. Farris co-founded the Home School Legal Defense Association (HSLDA), later founded Patrick Henry College, and eventually became president and CEO of the Alliance Defending Freedom (ADF), a Christian legal powerhouse.

The ADF helped draft and defend the Mississippi abortion law that led to the overturning of *Roe v. Wade*. It has filed lawsuits across the country claiming public schools violate parental and religious rights. The group is closely aligned with The Heritage Foundation, which launched Moms for Liberty, and sits on the advisory board of Project 2025, a far-right blueprint to consolidate executive power under the current president.

So when we say, "look behind the curtain," we're not being metaphorical.

The same groups behind the push to ban books are behind efforts to restrict abortion, erase LGBTQ+ rights, and dismantle public education. This isn't about libraries. It's about control.

They fear imagination.

They fear questions.

They fear kids who think for themselves.

We don't.

We know which side of the curtain we're on.

PART THREE

TEACHERS ON BOOK BANNING

11

"Amputate the Problem, Band-Aid the Solution": Censoring Toni Morrison

Amardeep Singh

The most commonly censored speakers and writers in the US are people from marginalized groups whose voices and arguments threaten state authority or the status quo. Books by Toni Morrison, especially *The Bluest Eye* and *Beloved*, regularly appear on the American Library Association's annual "10 Most Challenged" Lists, with *The Bluest Eye* in particular catching the attention of ban-oriented groups over the past few years. *The Bluest Eye,* a book published in 1970, was on the 10 most challenged books of 2022 and 2023[1], alongside very contemporary books like *Gender Queer* and *All Boys Aren't Blue.*

---

[1] American Library Association, "Top 10 Most Challenged Books of 2023." https://www.ala.org/bbooks/frequentlychallengedbooks/top10/archive.

As of this writing, the ALA does not yet appear to have published the most challenged books of 2024, but it is fully expected that Toni Morrison will again make an appearance.

As I have been teaching courses on Toni Morrison's fiction to undergraduates at my university, I have wanted to bring the library challenge campaigns to their attention, and possibly construct assignments inviting students to investigate the claims against Morrison's novels. The English paper prompt essentially writes itself: *What is the argument against Morrison in these complaints, and how would you respond?* Unfortunately, responding to this prompt has proved to be difficult, as the complainants don't actually present *arguments* as such. One of the people who filed a complaint against *The Bluest Eye*, Amber Crawford of the St. Charles Parents' Association in Wentzville, Missouri, simply listed "pediphilia [sic], incest, rape" as a sufficient reason[2].

It would be too generous to call this list of words an actual argument. Crawford's objection, like many others that have appeared around the US in recent years often uses cookie-cutter language pasted from the same lists online, and reduces Morrison's complex narrative to these three words as evidence of its "obscenity." Since the complainants in the thousands of school board censorship events typically do not read the books they're censoring, their complaints don't really constitute teachable moments.

Unfortunately, the lack of coherence does not necessarily help when it comes to defending Morrison's books. In the case of the Wentzville

---

[2]Wentzville School District Committee Report, January 13, 2022. The document quotes explicit passages from the novel, and then simply lists the rationale for objection as "pediphilia [sic], incest, rape." Accessed via the ACLU website: https://www.aclu.org/wp-content/uploads/legal-documents/Exhibit_5:_Committee_Decision_on_The_Bluest_Eye.

School District, the School Board voted to remove all copies of *The Bluest Eye* from school library shelves in January 2022; this was the first time a book had ever been removed from library shelves in this School district[3]. The ACLU filed suit in February, and shortly thereafter the School Board rescinded its ban of *The Bluest Eye*[4]. After the ban was lifted, however, six other books dealing primarily with LBGTQ+ themes remained banned.

If complainants did read the novel, they might after all be troubled: what's troubling in *The Bluest Eye* is actually its portrayal of young Black girls coming of age in a midwestern town at a time of total mass media and institutional erasure of Black bodies and experiences. What's really unsettling about the book is the way it tells the story of a child desperate to be loved, to be cared for—and who never finds that love. What is the impact of these painful messages on young people? What is the right age to read *The Bluest Eye*? That might be an interesting conversation to have; too bad we can't have it.

Of course, it's not only *The Bluest Eye* that has been targeted by censorious right wing activists. In the Virginia gubernatorial campaign of 2021, Glenn Youngkin's campaign showed an ad featuring a white woman (Laura Murphy, a conservative activist) complain about how her son had been assigned the novel *Beloved* in a high school English class, which according to her, contained "some of the most explicit material you can imagine."[5] The ad reignited a controversy that began

---

[3]Sruthi Ramesh, "WSD Bans Book, Deeming the Selection Inappropriate" *LHS Today*, January 31, 2022. Accessed online here: https://lhstoday.org/31945/news/wsd-bans-book-deeming-the-selection-inappropriate/.

[4]Associated Press, "Missouri District Rescinds Decision to Ban Toni Morrison Book." February 27, 222. NBC News. https://www.nbcnews.com/news/nbcblk/missouri-district-rescinds-decision-ban-toni-morrison-book-rcna17858.

[5]Glenn Youngkin Campaign Ad, October 25, 2021. X. https://x.com/GlennYoungkin/status/1452668527358402582.

in 2016, when Virginia lawmakers—on Laura Murphy's request—passed a law (widely referred to in the press as the "*Beloved* Bill") requiring schools to give parents advance warnings when explicit materials might show up in class, and also to provide less-explicit alternatives[6]. The governor at the time, Terry McAuliffe, vetoed the bill. It's unclear how important the ad was in moving voters, but it's worth acknowledging that Glenn Youngkin won that race and is, as of this writing, the sitting governor of Virginia.

Dana A. Williams, who has been President of the Toni Morrison Society as well as a Dean of the Graduate School at Howard University, historicized the present wave of censorship as part of a backlash against African American progress: "After the Black Lives Matter movement, after the 1619 Project, after the election of Barack Obama, any major moment in history where you see progress of people of color—Black people in particular—backlash will follow."[7] Morrison herself thought there was a connection. As she put it in her 2009 essay, "Peril," "Efforts to censor, starve, regulate and annihilate us are clear signs that something important has taken place."[8]

As we see a flood of right-wing censorious legislation, it is hard not to think that any indications that "something important has taken place" in recent years have been overwhelmed by that backlash.

---

[6]Chantal Winstead, "The 'Beloved' Bill: The Controversy of HB 516." April 24, 2016. *National Council of Teachers of English.* https://ncte.org/report/the-beloved-bill-the-controversy-of-hb-516/.

[7]Olivia B. Waxman, "Why Toni Morrison's Books Are So Often the Target of Book Bans." *Time,* January 31, 2022. https://time.com/6143127/toni-morrison-book-bans/.

[8]Toni Morrison, "Peril." In Toni Morrison, Ed. *Burn This Book: PEN Writers Speak Out on the Power of the Word.* New York: Harper, 2009.

Arguably, the wave of local school districts banning particular Toni Morrison books has been superseded by a massive wave of state-level laws banning any potentially sensitive topics related to race, gender, or sexuality at all. Ten states have passed such laws, and there have been more than 100 separate bills introduced across 33 different states. The language of state laws like the one passed in Oklahoma remains vague ("not one cent of taxpayer money should be used to define and divide young Oklahomans about their race or sex")[9], but they are interpreted by local school districts in very specific ways that lead to the banning of myriad books that deal with race or racism from the curriculum.

Morrison was consistent throughout her career in supporting the rights of writers to be controversial and to leave the reader troubled and unsettled. In her essay "Peril" from 2009, from the collection *Burn This Book*, she talked about the way censorship aims to impose statist language on the population:

Writers—journalists, essayists, bloggers, poets, playwrights—can disturb the social oppression that functions like a coma on the population, a coma despots call peace; and they stanch the blood flow of war that hawks and profiteers thrill to.

(Toni Morrison, "Peril")

It is hard to read this and not wonder what Morrison would say about the "blood flow of war" of our own era, of the vast curtain of censorship

---

[9]Anita Little, "On the Frontlines of the Fight Against Classroom Censorship." ACLU Website, September 15, 2023. https://www.aclu.org/news/free-speech/teachers-frontlines-classroom-censorship.

that has been descending on college campuses over the use of certain words or phrases related to Palestinians. Here's more from Morrison:

> The thought that leads me to contemplate with dread the erasure of other voices, of unwritten novels, poems whispered or swallowed for fear of being overheard by the wrong people, outlawed languages flourishing underground, essayists' questions challenging authority never being posed, unstaged plays, canceled films—that thought is a nightmare. As though a whole universe is being described in invisible ink.
>
> (Toni Morrison, "Peril")

Back in 1996, Morrison also wrote a powerful defense of a novel she clearly felt ambivalent about, Mark Twain's *Huckleberry Finn*. As is well-known, that novel has sometimes been banned or pulled from curricula on account of Twain's language. For Morrison, the use of the n-word in the book was never the problem, and she clearly condemned the efforts to have the book banned for that reason:

> It struck me as a purist yet elementary kind of censorship designed to appease adults rather than educate children. Amputate the problem, band-aid the solution. A serious comprehensive discussion of the term by an intelligent teacher certainly would have benefited my eighth-grade class and would have spared all of us (a few blacks, many whites—mostly second-generation immigrant children) some grief.
>
> (Toni Morrison, "Introduction" to *The Oxford Mark Twain: Adventures of Huckleberry Finn*, 1996)[10]

---

[10]Toni Morrison, "Introduction" to *The Oxford Mark Twain: Adventures of Huckleberry Finn*, edited by Shelley Fisher Fishkin. Oxford University Press, 1996.

All of this sounds like an incredibly apt description of what state legislatures are doing in their own ham-fisted censorship efforts at the present moment. (One does wonder, again, what Morrison would think about the idea of new editions of Twain where racial slurs have been swapped out—where the word "slave" is used instead of the word Twain himself used?[11])

Morrison's most profound discussion of the perils of censorship was perhaps her moving, challenging Nobel Prize Lecture from 1993. Here she tells a parable of a blind woman and young people who come to her to test her—is the bird in our hands living or dead? Her response, as many readers will remember, is: "I don't know whether the bird you are holding is dead or alive, but what I do know is that it is in your hands. It is in your hands." Morrison goes on to interpret the bird in the inquisitors' hands as *language*—what will we do with it? Will we let it live? Will we kill it just to win the rhetorical point?

Some of Morrison's most thoughtful and moving arguments against censorship from her entire career follow. There are two main threads: one follows from the bird in hand parable; the other speaks to the question of hate speech. In both cases, Morrison's rhetoric seems remarkably prescient for a text more than thirty years old. She is keenly attuned to the alignment between repressive language and institutional authority, as we see here:

For her a dead language is not only one no longer spoken or written, it is unyielding language content to admire its own paralysis. Like

---

[11]Benedicte Page, "New Huckleberry Finn edition censors 'n-word.'" *The Guardian*, January 5, 2011. https://www.theguardian.com/books/2011/jan/05/huckleberry-finn-edition-censors-n-word.

statist language, censored and censoring. Ruthless in its policing duties, it has no desire or purpose other than maintaining the free range of its own narcotic narcissism, its own exclusivity and dominance. However moribund, it is not without effect for it actively thwarts the intellect, stalls conscience, suppresses human potential. Unreceptive to interrogation, it cannot form or tolerate new ideas, shape other thoughts, tell another story, fill baffling silences. Official language smitheryed to sanction ignorance and preserve privilege is a suit of armor polished to shocking glitter, a husk from which the knight departed long ago. Yet there it is: dumb, predatory, sentimental. Exciting reverence in schoolchildren, providing shelter for despots, summoning false memories of stability, harmony among the public.

(Toni Morrison, Nobel Lecture, 1993, n.p.)

For Morrison, censorious language is a kind of dead zone, antithetical to creativity ("it cannot form or tolerate new ideas [...] tell another story"). Censorship need not be pegged to a specific bad actor; in censorious climates it seems to infect language and thought ("censored and censoring") so that one may not be entirely sure where the censorship originated, or where anticipatory compliance in the form self-censorship ends and state repression begins. And the vacuum it produces is a key component of the false sense of order that can be imposed in totalitarian regimes.

Here is another key moment where Morrison appears to anticipate the sins of the censorious 2020s from the vantage point of the early 1990s:

The systematic looting of language can be recognized by the tendency of its users to forgo its nuanced, complex, mid-wifery properties for menace and subjugation. Oppressive language does more than represent violence; it is violence; does more than represent the limits of knowledge; it limits knowledge. Whether it is obscuring state language or the faux-language of mindless media; whether it is the proud but calcified language of the academy or the commodity driven language of science; whether it is the malign language of law-without-ethics, or language designed for the estrangement of minorities, hiding its racist plunder in its literary cheek – it must be rejected, altered and exposed. It is the language that drinks blood, laps vulnerabilities, tucks its fascist boots under crinolines of respectability and patriotism as it moves relentlessly toward the bottom line and the bottomed-out mind. Sexist language, racist language, theistic language – all are typical of the policing languages of mastery, and cannot, do not permit new knowledge or encourage the mutual exchange of ideas.

(Toni Morrison, Nobel Lecture, 1993, n.p.)

The alignment of a critique of mass media ("mindless media"), the capitalist profit-motive and the evacuation of thought ("the bottom line and the bottomed-out mind") is one that has, in our present era of social media oligarchy, become even more prevalent and pernicious. Morrison, at the peak of her fame and at a moment of institutional triumph in Sweden, could see it all coming.

Today's school board book ban campaigners and state legislators disallowing discussions of race, gender, and sexuality—as inherently subversive of the lily-white, heroic model of American history—are doing exactly what Morrison describes. They are enacting, through erasure, the violence of a statist narrative in which racism and slavery, misogyny and homophobia, have been minor historical aberrations, not a defining story. But Morrison was also insistent that such attempts at censorship can be vigorously resisted (repressive language "must be rejected, altered and exposed"). No matter what the school board attempts to do—or the Governor, or the President—Toni Morrison's fiction can and will be read.

12
Banned Books in Transnational Contexts: Censorship in School Curricula in Wisconsin and India

Lopamudra Basu

The topic of banned books, when discussed in the US, tends to remain restricted to book challenges occurring within the national boundaries of the United States. However, the banning of books is not just a US phenomenon but something occurring in a transnational context. From the perspective of my own biography, my earliest encounter with books being banned was with Salman Rushdie's *The Satanic Verses* in India in 1988. India had the dubious distinction of being the first country to ban this novel, which arguably galvanized international attention leading to the fatwa issued on Rushdie by the Iranian Supreme Leader Ayatollah Khomeini. That decree resulted in Rushdie's having to live in hiding for many years and culminated in his shocking stabbing in Chautauqua, New York which nearly took his life in 2022. The banning of *The Satanic Verses* in India in my youth and the attack on Rushdie's life in New York more than three decades later are the two sensational events bookending my scholarly interest in book banning.

In the interim between these two moments, a lot has happened in both my natal and adopted countries. The state where I live and teach is Wisconsin, which has one of the highest numbers of books banned or challenged. Since 2021, at least 451 books have been banned in the state.[1] While book banning in Wisconsin does not approximate the high drama of the Rushdie Affair or assassination attempt, there are some common threads which I hope to uncover in this chapter. While many books have been challenged in Wisconsin, the two that I will focus on are *When the Emperor Was Divine* by Julie Otsuka and *I Am Malala* by Malala Yousafzai, which faced challenges in two different school districts in Wisconsin. What connects them to the continuing rise in book bans in India in recent decades is that, in both national contexts, banning stems from the fear of minority histories and cultures by increasingly authoritarian state structures supported by racial and ethnic majorities. In this essay, I reflect both on examples of books being removed from Wisconsin schools and on the limiting of Islamic history content in high schools in India. I connect these examples of censorship separated by geography to the worldwide growth of ethno-nationalisms and deep discomfort with

---

[1]Markham, Madison and Tessalyn Magnusson (2024), "The State of Book Bans: Wisconsin's Battle with Parental Rights," 18 July. https://pen.org/the-state-of-book-bans-wisconsins-battle-with-parental-rights/.

aspects of history that do not conform to a mythology of a monolithic and uncontested past.

First, I would like to focus on the book challenge faced by Julie Otsuka's novel in a specific school district in Wisconsin. Otsuka's 2002 novel *When the Emperor Was Divine* was selected by southeastern Wisconsin's Muskego-Norway district curriculum committee, but rejected in 2022 by the Muskego-Norway School Board for a 10th grade accelerated English course. Even though school district residents, under the auspices of the Asian Pacific Islander Coalition of Wisconsin, organized in favor of the book, at the date of this writing the novel remains banned from the 10th grade curriculum.

The reason offered for the removal of Otsuka's novel was that it needed to be paired with another work that presented the other side: the American justification of the internment of its citizens of Japanese origin. This appeal to "balance" stemmed from the inclusion in the 10th grade curriculum of a ten-page excerpt of *Farewell to Manzanar,* a 1973 memoir by Jeanne Wakatsuki Houston and James D. Houston about their internment experience in California. Kandice Chuh asserts that the "charge of imbalance stems from the absence of a US government perspective contextualizing internment against the bombing of Pearl Harbor, a charge that reproduces the racially essentialist assumption of Japanese American loyalties to Japan that rationalized internment".[2]

---

[2]Chuh, Kandice. "Too Sad, Too Diverse, Too Poetic." *PMLA/Publications of the Modern Language Association of America* 138, no. 1 (2023): 218–22. https://doi.org/10.1632/S0030812923000056.

Other reasons cited for the book's rejection included that the novel was "too sad" "too diverse" and "too poetic." In examining these charges, Chuh points to the "calculus of quantity, affect, and national interest that rationalizes text selection."[3] She argues that the Wisconsin example is one of hundreds of examples of curricular contests happening nationally around works that focus on criticism of the US or foreground themes of racism and sexuality. Such contests over curriculum can be traced back to at least the Civil War and are rooted in "the centrality of whiteness and cis-heteronormativity in the nation's self-fashioning."[4]

Even closer to my home, another controversy that erupted in 2017 was the inclusion of *I Am Malala* in the 8th grade English curriculum of Menomonie Middle School. Menomonie is the location of University of Wisconsin-Stout, where I teach. This was the second year the book had been assigned and a speaker from an Islamic Resource Center in Minneapolis came to the 8th grade classroom to discuss Islam, which is central to understanding Malala's life and work as a practicing Muslim. The visit prompted a complaint by one parent of a student in Jason Collins's class, which led to a public discussion at a school board meeting of April 24, 2017. This meeting included an agenda item to consider complaints against specific persons in closed session. The Chippewa Valley chapter of ACLU, in a letter to Superintendent Zydowsky of the School District of Menomonie Area, questioned the appeasement of individual parents for complaints about their children's curriculum with closed sessions devoted to complaining. The ACLU's letter expresses support for Collins for his decision to

---

[3] Chuh, "Too Sad," 221.
[4] Ibid., 219.

include knowledge about Islam in his curriculum and for Ms. Stacy Everson, Menomonie Middle School Principal, for supporting Mr. Collins's decision to teach the book *I Am Malala*.

In spite of ACLU's strong support of Collins's decision to teach *I Am Malala* and questioning of the District's handling of parental complaints, the higher administration continued with their policy and actions of parental appeasement. In spite of a community forum on May 15, 2017, attended by 150 people, in which a large number of parents spoke in favor of introducing children to diverse religions, and in spite of the Board determining that nothing illegal had occurred in the visit by a Muslim speaker to an 8th grade classroom, the Board determined to have the curriculum reviewed in advance to make sure that religion was being taught in an appropriate manner. In the following year, parents would have the option to request alternative assignments if they were not comfortable with their children listening to any speaker.[5] The ACLU, in the same public letter to the Superintendent, where they supported Collins, questioned the effectiveness of the decision to allow alternative assignments in future years.

As a result of this aggressive parental pushback against *I Am Malala*, principal Stacy Everson quit and relocated. In subsequent years, teachers including Collins have steered clear of teaching this book. Collins also faced some backlash for his determination to continue teaching this book. During the pandemic he chose to teach online; once the pandemic ended, he faced difficulty in returning to

---

[5]Powers, Pamela (2017) "Menomonie School District to Review the Role of Religion in Curriculum." Leader Telegram, 25 April. Available online: https://www.leadertelegram.com/news/front-page/menomonie-school-district-to-review-role-of-religion-in-curriculum/article_a3a53943-ca80-5655-8c2d-15973de7a54d.html.

the middle school due to the decision by the school to consolidate positions. He is grateful that a last-minute resignation allowed him to get hired at Menomonie High School, where he currently teaches. He feels that the middle school environment no longer supports a curriculum like his that included *I Am Malala*.

In comparing these two cases, it is easy to see the common tension between the inclusion of racial and cultural diversity and parental opposition. Parental opposition is voiced in the Muskego-Norway episode in the complaint by Board members that the curriculum was becoming too slanted in favor of minority perspectives. In the case of the Menomonie school district, parental opposition stems from the appearance of a Muslim speaker to contextualize a memoir by a Muslim woman. In both cases, parental opposition is presented as a need for balance and an assertion of parental rights to monitor and limit access to the school district's curriculum.

While these challenges are presented as legitimate concerns of parents, further investigation debunks the idea that these campaigns are spontaneous grassroots efforts to counter what is perceived as unilateral decisions by school districts. The opposition to diversity in school curricula must be viewed within the wider context of political opposition to Critical Race Theory and Diversity, Equity and Inclusion initiatives nationwide, even before the advent of the second Trump administration. While states beyond Florida have instituted laws like the Stop Woke Act, Wisconsin has faced a record number of book challenges; in 2024, the Democratic governor vetoed a Parental Rights bill.[6] Markham and Magnusson argue that Parental Rights bills like AB 510 comprise

---

[6]Markham and Magnusson.

what PEN America has described as "educational intimidation." If we examine the statements made by the Muskego-Norway Board members who decided in a meeting to remove Julie Otsuka's novel from the curriculum, some of these same currents come into play.

Terri Boyer, Chair of the School Board at Muskego-Norway, said she was worried the book was chosen because of the identity of the author, a Japanese American.[7] At the meeting Laurie Kontney, newest Board member, said "They only looked at diverse books." When pressed by a parent, she said "it cannot be all about oppression."[8] Kontney was elected on a platform of "Critical Thinking Not Critical Race Theory" and "Learning Free of Political Influence." The use of the slogan "Critical Thinking Not Critical Race Theory" in this episode provides us a key to understanding what is going on with book bans in schools in the US. The American Library Association in 2021 recorded 729 challenges against 1597 books. PEN America reported 1586 bans during this period.[9] The majority of challengers were parents or patrons. They were against BIPOC and LGBTQIA works. ALA reports that in 2021, every title in the Top 10 most challenged books either had so-called anti-police views, LGBTQIA+ content, or a label of "sexually explicit."[10]

---

[7]Linane, Rory (2022). "Wisconsinites Rally Around Book Rejected by Muskego Board for Focus on Japanese Experience." *Milwaukee Journal Sentinel*, 18 July. https://eu.jsonline.com/story/news/education/2022/07/18/rally-backs-book-rejected-muskego-focus-japanese-americans/10051434002/.

[8]Lueders, Bill (2022), "Wisconsin School District Rejects Book About Japanese Internment." *Wisconsin Examiner*, 22 June. https://wisconsinexaminer.com/2022/06/22/wisconsin-school-district-rejects-book-about-japanese-internment.

[9]Oltmann, Shannon. M (2023), "Libraries in the 2020s" in Shannon M. Oltmann (ed), *The Fight Against Book Bans: Perspectives from the Field*, 1–7, New York: Bloomsbury.

[10]Oltmann, "Libraries."

Glen J. Benedict, in her essay "It's Not Just the Quantity: Book Challenges in 2021 and Beyond" (collected in Shannon Oltman's anthology *The Fight Against Book Bans: Perspectives from the Field*), explains the difference between grassroots organizing and astroturfing in the context of parental groups supporting book bans: "astroturfing, as a concept, refers to the use of grassroots aesthetics in political organizing to pose an illusion of organic, unprompted, or populist support."

Three major organizations, Moms for Liberty, No Left Turn in Education, and Parents Defending Education, each refer to themselves as a grassroots organization or movement. However, a closer look at each reveals deep connections to powerful political figures and institutions. Benedict uncovers ties of these groups to Republican elected officials and donors like the Koch Brothers. These parental rights movements are not spontaneous grassroots movements responding to local issues, but rather well-organized and well-funded initiatives often directed from outside the specific locations where the controversies are being played out. If we apply Benedict's research on these parental rights groups to the events in Muskego-Norway, we can see a clear connection between the contesting of School Board elections and decisions to restrict diversity content. Laurie Kontney won her seat in the Muskego-Norway School District on a platform to restrict Critical Race Theory; her vociferous opposition to *When the Emperor was Divine* fulfilled her campaign stance against diversity content. School board elections have become high-stakes contests in the era of book banning. In the Menomonie School District, the *I Am Malala* controversy and its repercussions on a teacher and a principal prompted more progressives, including university professors, to campaign for—and win—School Board elections.

Besides contesting school board elections, communities like Muskego-Norway have organized to resist attempts to restrict access to books. Julie Otsuka in an interview said,

> The school board's attempt to whitewash history was met with fierce opposition by local parents, students, and high school alumni. Over 300 people signed a petition urging the school board to reconsider […] Money was raised to purchase and distribute 100 free copies of my novel; there were rallies and teach-ins … and this in a deeply conservative town … it was a beautiful thing to watch.
>
> (Otsuka qtd in Glatman, 2023)

However, in spite of these efforts, the book has not yet made it to the 10th Grade Accelerated English program. Popular movements cannot completely undo ravages to the school curriculum by Boards averse to multicultural content.

Book bans in India since the 1980s have occurred on a much larger scale: the banning of novels like Salman Rushdie's *The Satanic Verses* in 1988 was enacted by the Congress government under pressure from Muslim leaders, ostensibly to prevent communal violence. This was later seen as minority appeasement by the BJP, the party of the Hindu Right. In an ironic reversal, the ban on *The Satanic Verses* in effect from 1988 was lifted in November 2024, after a petitioner asked to see the original ban and it could not be produced by the Delhi High Court. This has resulted in the novel being imported to India after more than three decades. Rushdie's *The Moor's Last Sigh* was banned in the state of Maharashtra in 1995 and Rohinton Mistry's *Such a Long Journey* dropped from the Bombay University syllabus in 2010. Mistry's book is particularly relevant since it was dropped because of its negative portrayal of the Shiv Sena, a militant wing of the Hindu Right. The complaint was brought forth by Aditya Thackeray who was then a student at the university and objected to the negative portrayal of his grandfather Bal Thackeray, a founding leader of Shiv Sena. This incident clearly replicates the script of educational intimidation that we have seen playing out in Wisconsin schools.

Under the BJP, we have seen recent attacks on texts of Indian history written by western scholars including Joseph Lelyveld's *The Great Soul: Mahatma Gandhi and His Struggle with India,* and Wendy Doniger's *The Hindus; An Alternative History.* The steady stream of attacks faced by these authors culminated in Doniger's publisher Penguin India pulping all copies of her book.

In India, censorship is not restricted to books and educational institutions. Some of the most egregious acts of censorship and harassment have been directed towards filmmakers. Indo-Canadian filmmaker Deepa Mehta faced censorship in connection with two of her films *Fire* and *Water.* In the case of *Fire,* on December 2, 1998, members of the Mahila Aghadi (the women's wing of the Shiv Sena) marched into a theatre in Mumbai where *Fire* was being screened and smashed glass panes, destroyed posters, and shouted slogans. Similar episodes followed in cities like Delhi and Pune with Shiv Sena women engaging in arson. The ostensible reason for these actions were that these groups from the Hindu Right were protesting against the depiction of a lesbian relationship in *Fire.* According to

Madhu Jain and Sheela Raval, there was "a method in the madness—a hooliganism that had state protection".[11] A few years later, when Deepa Mehta was filming *Water* in Varanasi, her sets were vandalized, and she was forced to stop production. Once again, it was the Shiv Sena that attacked her sets as *Water* was purportedly going to present a negative image of Hindu widowhood. Mehta later completed the film in Sri Lanka in secret.

The hooliganism of the foot soldiers of the Hindu Right has not been limited to film productions. Visual artist M. F. Hussain had his apartment vandalized in 1998 for his painting of nude Sita, the heroine of the Hindu epic *Ramayana*.

Although the violent disruptions of film screenings and production tend to make more headlines, the most consequential acts of censorship are those occurring more insidiously in Indian history textbooks. The National Council of Educational Research and Training, which produces textbooks to be used all over India, has quietly deleted large sections of medieval Indian history centered around Muslim dynasties like the Mughals. The latest deletions in NCERT textbooks are not just limited to omissions of large sections of Mughal history. The name of the assassin of Mahatma Gandhi, Nathuram Godse, and his affiliation with the Hindu Right has also been omitted. Romila Thapar also points out that the NCERT textbooks are silent about the Muslim pogroms in Gujerat in 2002. She argues, "these events survive as part of social memory and are

---

[11]Raval, Sheela, and Madhu Jain (1998), "Deepa Mehta's Film Fire Creates a Furore" *India Today*, 21 December. https://www.indiatoday.in/magazine/society-the-arts/films/story/19981221-controversial-film-fire-is-sent-back-to-censor-board-matter-taken-to-court-827561-1998-12-20.

spoken of both publicly and in quietude. They become the subject of other books and debates and are not forgotten."[11] Thapar deconstructs the idea of a monolithic Hinduism; she provides detailed evidence-based examples to repudiate the narrative of Hindu victimization propagated by the Hindu Right to strongly oppose the deletion of significant sections of Mughal history from high school textbooks.

While in the US cases of censorship play out at the local school board level, in India, where education is more centralized, we are witnessing the disappearance of Muslim history from school textbooks without any recourse to the protests or teach-ins and organizing seen in Wisconsin. Unless the political climate and the supremacy of the Hindu Right weakens electorally, there is little chance of restoration of a less monolithic presentation of Indian history. The comparative analysis of specific cases of books banned in schools in Wisconsin and India show that they stem from similar anxieties about national identity and from insistence on erasing minority histories in the public sphere. Even though access to diversity in school curricula can be temporarily restricted, knowledge of our complex and multicultural pasts cannot be obliterated. With changes in electoral power, locally in the case of Wisconsin or at the national level in India, these curricular damages can, I hope, be reversed.

---

[11] Thapar, Romila (2023), Our *History, Their History, Whose History*. Calcutta: Seagull: 133.

13

Illiberal Education

Annie Abrams

On July 21, 2009, Bill Gates addressed the National Conference of State Legislatures. Urging policymakers to adopt the Common Core State Standards, developed by a company called Achieve and a group called the National Governor's Association, he promised a renaissance in American curricular quality:

> When the tests are aligned to the common standards, the curriculum will line up as well—and that will unleash powerful market forces in the service of better teaching. For the first time, there will be a large base of customers eager to buy products that can help every kid learn and every teacher get better. Imagine having the people who create electrifying video games applying their intelligence to online tools.[1]

---

[1] Bill Gates, "Prepared Remarks, National Conference of State Legislatures (NCSL)." Gates Foundation, July 20, 2009. https://www.gatesfoundation.org/Ideas/Speeches/2009/07/bill-gates-national-conference-of-state-legislatures-ncsl.

Under centralized, streamlined national standards, scale and profit would incentivize inventive, ambitious entrepreneurs. In *The Bill Gates Problem*, Tim Schwab described this approach to education in terms of "monopoly logic."[2] In 2014, the *Washington Post* reported that, in Gates's view, "one of the benefits of common standards would be to open the classroom to digital learning, making it easier for software developers—including Microsoft—to develop new products for the country's 15,000 school districts."[3]

The Common Core's emphasis on raising academic expectations through curricular prescriptions sparked debates about what students should read in schools, and who gets to decide such things. The Standards drew a sharp distinction between "informational" and "literary" texts. A mandate that 70% of a student's readings, across the curriculum, should be nonfiction by 12th grade set off alarm bells. Even an *LA Times* defense of the standards warned, "no matter how the designers of the new curriculum intended it to be carried out, as a practical matter, English teachers will probably end up taking on a disproportionate responsibility for this new emphasis on nonfiction," and concluded that as "a panel of education experts" in California started to align English curricula with the standards, the group should resist "the temptation to translate the standards into a rigid mandate that reduces students' exposure to the richly engaging, imaginative

---

[2]Tim Schwab, *The Bill Gates Problem : Reckoning with the Myth of the Good Billionaire*. First edition. New York: Metropolitan Books, Henry Holt and Company, 2023.

[3]Lynsey Layton, "How Bill Gates pulled off the swift Common Core revolution," *The Washington Post*, June 7, 2014, http://www.washingtonpost.com/politics/how-bill-gates-pulled-off-the-swift-common-core-revolution/2014/06/07/a830e32e-ec34-11e3-9f5c-9075d5508f0a_story.html.

and thought-provoking world of fiction and poetry."[4] Diane Ravitch argued, "There is no reason for national standards to tell teachers what percentage of their time should be devoted to literature or information."[5] Betsy Woodruff warned, "The greater problem here is the premise behind the change: that students read so they can learn how to process information and eventually get jobs as information processors."[6] Indeed, Rex Tillerson championed the new standards on the basis that public schools "exist to serve" corporations.[7]

In the *Huffington Post*, Common Core's English Language Arts architects David Coleman and Susan Pimentel rejected arguments that the Core would disincentivize literature instruction. Even as they acknowledged "the expansion of high-quality literary nonfiction in ELA," including a new requirement for English teachers to cover "our country's Founding Documents and the 'Great Conversation' they inspired," they insisted, "the Standards in no way ask ELA teachers to abandon literature; instead, they require that students read demanding, high-quality fiction and demonstrate their ability to analyze such fiction."[8] In promotional materials and media reports, the Common Core's proselytizers promised that under the new regime,

---

[4] "What Students Read," *Los Angeles Times*, December 27, 2012, https://www.latimes.com/opinion/editorials/la-xpm-2012-dec-27-la-ed-1227-fiction-20121227-story.html.

[5] Diane Ravitch, "Why I Oppose Common Core Standards," *The Washington Post*, February 26, 2013, https://www.washingtonpost.com/news/answer-sheet/wp/2013/02/26/why-i-oppose-common-core-standards-ravitch/.

[6] Betsy Woodruff, "Goodby Liberal Arts?" *The National Review*, December 13, 2012, https://www.nationalreview.com/2012/12/goodbye-liberal-arts-betsy-woodruff/.

[7] Peter Elkind, "How Business Got Schooled," *Fortune Magazine*, December 23, 2015, https://fortune.com/longform/common-core-standards/.

[8] David Coleman and Susan Pimentel, "The Role of Fiction in the High School English Language Arts Classroom," *The Huffington Post*, December 11, 2012, https://www.huffpost.com/entry/the-role-of-fiction-in-th_b_2279782.

students would be "college and career-ready," and that tests and other forms of external control would ensure skill acquisition. Despite these assurances, backlash to consolidated control over curriculum was loud and swift, across the political spectrum. The "Common Core" brand became so radioactive that by the mid-2010s, many states that had adopted the Common Core Standards had renamed them, even as they maintained their substance and mechanisms for implementation and enforcement.[9]

This chapter considers the role of books in the Common Core framework and the meaning of book bans within this broader policy frame. Book bans come amidst a broad turn away from liberal education, across school and college.

Despite the education reform movement's ubiquitous promises of "college and career readiness," in October 2024, *The Atlantic's* Rose Horowitch challenged the notion that current state standards adequately prepare high school students for undergraduate education. She reported on English professors' sense that many of their students were arriving on campus incapable of reading long, ambitious works of literature. Citing conversations with veteran teachers, she wrote, "For more than two decades, new educational initiatives such as No Child Left Behind and Common Core emphasized informational texts and standardized tests. Teachers at many schools shifted from books to short informational passages, followed by questions about the author's main idea—mimicking the format of standardized reading-

---

[9]Elkind, "How Business Got Schooled".

comprehension tests."[10] To be sure, what teacher and consultant Kelly Gallagher termed "readicide" existed in schools long before Common Core.[11] But the new tests worsened rather than ameliorated the problem. One example is a change to the New York State Regents exam: prior to adoption of a Common Core model requiring students to write two or three paragraphs about literary devices in a short provided passage, they were expected to write essays citing two works of literature to form an argument about a controversial statement. Despite New York State's shift from "Common Core" to "Next Generation Learning Standards" in name, in practice, the test has not returned to assessing literary knowledge.

Horowitch's critique builds on others that have blamed the standards for desiccating literature instruction. New College of Florida Board Trustee Mark Bauerlein quote-tweeted her article on X: "Reminder that Common Core emphasized close reading of short passages more than complete reading of long books." Robert Pondiscio, an American Enterprise Institute fellow and frequent champion of the Core, complained about a model lesson and aligned curriculum in 2014: "Excerpts. No complete works. Bleeding chunks of literature chosen because they presumably offer opportunities to learn and practice a reading 'skill.'"[12] In 2018, former teacher and education writer Peter Greene argued, "The Common Core Standards do not require reading complete long works of literature." He explained that students'

---

[10]Rose Horwitch, "The Elite College Students Who Can't Read Books," *The Atlantic*, October 1, 2024, https://www.theatlantic.com/magazine/archive/2024/11/the-elite-college-students-who-cant-read-books/679945/.

[11]Kelly Gallagher, *Readicide* New York: Routledge, 2009.

[12]Robert Pondiscio, "A Missed Opportunity for Common Core," Education Next, March 26, 2020, https://www.educationnext.org/missed-opportunity-common-core/.

experience of literature has been fractured and shrunk into pieces small enough to fit on a screen. Their experience of what 'reading' is has been shrunk as well, leaving them with the idea that reading is about ploughing through a short, disjointed piece of a piece of writing in order to correctly guess the answers about it that someone else believes are correct (based on the assumption that there is only one correct reading of each passage).[13]

Rightly, Greene admits that some teachers and schools have resisted the trend. But the policy frame subordinates considerations like literary merit, cultural significance, and pleasure to utility in terms of test preparation.

After Horowitch's piece went viral, the Fordham Institute's Michael Petrilli wrote a blog post entreating readers to blame neither Common Core nor "standardized testing and No Child Left Behind." He advised parents and educators concerned about literature's place in American curriculum to consult EdReports, arguing that "Education Reports could also do some good by only giving 'green' reviews to products that promote reading full-length works (which may also include plays, epic poems, biographies, and more)." Some profitable standards-aligned curriculum companies focus on excerpts: CommonLit promises "benchmark assessments," "actionable data," and "personalized webinars" based on short passages, with different prices per school based on tiered services.[14] But even top-down assignment of classic

---

[13]Peter Greene, "Common Core Testing and the Fracturing of Literature," Forbes, December 4, 2018, https://www.forbes.com/sites/petergreene/2018/11/09/common-core-testing-and-the-fracturing-of-literature/.

[14]*CommonLit.* https://www.commonlit.org/en (Accessed: February 25, 2025).

books distorts the purposes of assigning literature at scale in a free society. Harold Bloom's bestselling book on the Western canon—criticized by many on the left as exclusionary and hierarchical—lists 1,531 titles. But private vendors are poised to profit from sharper restriction, at scale.

Contests over curricular authority have long shaped American public education.[15] Currently, teachers' speech belongs to the state. In the words of the Seventh Circuit's Judge Easterbrook, "Expression is a teacher's stock in trade, the commodity she sells to her employer in exchange for a salary ... A high-school teacher hired to explicate *Moby-Dick* in a literature class can't use *Cry, The Beloved Country* instead, even if Paton's book better suits the instructor's style and point of view."[16] Administrators, school boards, and legislators can determine for a teacher what is worth teaching. Within the context of testing skills in the standards era, controls on the quality of the works students might encounter, and attempts to realize Gates's vision, can also come in the form of scripted curricula to which teachers are expected to adhere.

The Council of Chief State School Officers, according to its own website, a nonpartisan organization "of public officials who head departments of elementary and secondary education" is committed

---

[15]See, for example, Diana D'Amico Pawlewicz, *Blaming Teachers: Professionalization Policies and the Failure of Reform in American History* (New Brunswick, NJ: Rutgers University Press, 2020).; Nicholas Tampio, *Common Core: National Education Standards and the Threat to Democracy* (Baltimore: Johns Hopkins University Press, 2018); Jonathan Zimmerman, *Whose America?: Culture Wars in the Public Schools* (Chicago: University of Chicago Press, 2022).

[16]Mayer v. Monroe County Community School ..., accessed February 25, 2025, https://caselaw.findlaw.com/court/us-7th-circuit/1233551.html.

to tilting the implementation of curricula further in the direction of "a state-level policy consideration." In 2017, CCSSO and "a cohort of interested states launched the High-Quality Instructional Materials and Professional Development (IMPD) Network dedicated to ensuring that every student, every day, is engaged in meaningful, affirming, grade-level instruction." According to this logic, even greater degrees of curricular standardization, enforced by the state, could afford equality of opportunity. This group does not promote individual books on the basis of their aesthetic value: it emphasizes complete, scripted curricula aligned with tests.

The Texas Education Agency's recent takeover of the Houston Independent School District is an illustrative example of extreme emphasis on centralized state standards and testing, and curriculum and facilities designed primarily with these elements in mind. In July 2023, Mike Miles, the newly installed superintendent, announced that under his leadership, the schools would no longer employ librarians. As part of the takeover, he pledged to devote all available resources to increasing math and English test scores. Libraries would become "team centers," or "dual-purpose study halls for advanced students and detention centers for students sent out of class over discipline issues."[17] The district did not dispose of books: students could still borrow books on an honor system instead of formally checking them out. But concerned citizens have accused Miles of depriving students of space to read and to dream. The *Houston Landing* reported that at a

---

[17] "Library killer or book lover?" *Houston Chronicle*, accessed February 25, 2025, https://www.houstonchronicle.com/opinion/editorials/article/miles-hisd-houston-libraries-books-18340935.php.

board meeting, one speaker compared "the library conditions to Jim Crow."[18]

When the Houston Chronicle interviewed Miles about the issue, he said, "Let's think creatively. How about we have an AI-upgraded program. And we include online books for kids so they can easily, like … many adults, get books online? And read for free. You don't even need a library. How about we get the city to work with us to put up internet access for communities that are underserved?"[19] In December 2024, the system adopted AI-generated, standards-aligned reading passages from tech company Prof Jim to give "advanced" students additional test practice after meeting classroom benchmarks ahead of schedule, in what used to be the library. Miles's insistence on lessening reliance on books and physical spaces in which to enjoy them and increasing dependence on digital access to information takes the Common Core testing regime's imperatives to the extreme. In doing so, Miles reveals how books—the physical objects, and the narratives they hold—are, at best, extraneous to that project. One supportive principal told the *Houston Landing*, "It's not about having a library. It's about building students' love of literacy and appreciation for a book … That's what I feel like, this year, the (new) curriculum and even the (new) model encourages."[20] Others disagree with Miles's approach to management: over 10,000 employees have left the system over the past two years. Students have protested, and one took to

---

[18]Asher Lehrer-Small, "ARE HISD Students Checking out Fewer Books at Schools without Librarians? It's Hard to Say.," *Houston Landing*, February 20, 2024, https://houstonlanding. org/hisd-librarian-book-checkout-mike-miles-school-overhaul-nes/.
[19]"Library killer or book lover?".
[20]Lehrer-Small, "Are HISD Checking Out Fewer Books".

social media to explain that they "walked out because our library is used for everything but reading."[21]

Meanwhile, Texas Senate Bill 88, filed in November 2024 by Republican Senator Bob Hall, titled "Relating to the prosecution of the criminal offense of sale, distribution, or display of harmful material to a minor," seeks to change existing legislation around obscenity in school books. The prior version of the law, from 2011, requires "harmful material" to be considered in relation to a work's "dominant theme taken as a whole," and removing material required it to be "utterly" absent of "redeeming social value for minors." The new version strikes these qualifications, which means that if a book has any "sex, nudity, or excretion" at all, as many classics do, it could be prohibited in schools. If the law passes, anodyne AI-generated excerpts will remain safe.

Book challenges in Texas and other red states make headlines and capture national attention. But there are ways in which books' precarity in Democrat-controlled states and cities, like New York City's public schools, particularly in the lower grades, mirrors that in Houston. As part of New York City's literacy overhaul, former Chancellor David Banks required all public school districts to choose from among three test-aligned, standardized English Language Arts curricula. Only one of the programs—Wit and Wisdom—emphasizes multiple, complete works of fiction, and, even in schools using that curriculum, teachers cede autonomy and

---

[21]Books belong in school; attend read-in Thur—Community Voices for Public Education, accessed February 25, 2025, https://www.houstoncvpe.org/books_belong_in_school_attend_read_in_thur.

homegrown lesson plans to top-down test preparation. When Moms for Liberty complained about the curriculum's approach to covering race in Tennessee, a spokesperson for Great Minds, the curriculum company, said, "It's important to note that Wit & Wisdom is in full compliance with Tennessee state law."[22] The program is nationwide—it must comply with such laws even in states, like New York, where they do not exist. When Boston Public Schools, under increased pressure to raise state testing scores adopted the same program, elementary school teachers argued that it was "severely lacking in cultural relevance." In a letter to the Chancellor, they wrote, "At best, we would advocate to keep our autonomy and choose a curriculum that we know represents our students. At the least, we expect our district leaders to make a choice that does not blatantly perpetuate inequality."[23]

Currently, support for orienting cultural education towards standardized testing comes in the form of a turn from whole-language literacy programs to a new emphasis on phonics and "science of reading." Susan Neuman, an NYU Steinhardt professor who worked to implement No Child Left Behind as part of the Bush administration, has voiced support for New York City's initiative in *Chalkbeat* and the *New York Times*. "The whole idea behind this initiative is to lift the boats of the kids who have been traditionally left behind, and that

---

[22]Herald Reports, "Complaint Filed by Local Moms For Liberty Chapter Rejected by State," Williamson Herald, November 30, 2021, https://www.williamsonherald.com/features/education/complaint-filed-by-local-moms-for-liberty-chapter-rejected-by-state/article_81146dc4-518f-11ec-9d9a-237001a4ab9f.html.

[23]Schoolyard News, "Thirty-One Mission Hill School Faculty Protest Wit and Wisdom Curriculum," Medium, July 14, 2020, https://schoolyardnews.com/thirty-one-mission-hill-school-faculty-protest-wit-and-wisdom-curriculum-2e3b3abc4f8a.

means some of the advanced students might be subject to a simpler program," she explained. "Right now, that's the cost."[24] In agreement with this philosophy, Robert Carroll, a Democratic assemblyman from Brooklyn, called for "evidence-based practices" to be "implemented with fidelity."[25] In practice, this demand for "fidelity" entails compliance with curriculum teachers might find inadequate or too challenging. Some parents and teachers are protesting the changes in New York.[26] It's unclear why a switch to "science of reading" or phonics instruction necessitates standardization at this scale, eradicating classroom libraries, or disallowing teachers to choose the books they assign.[27]

✱✱✱

Under the reasonable, benign-sounding banners of nonpartisanship and science, technocratic, test-obsessed reformers are offering a politicized form of education: the current process of accreditation, with explicit economic ends in view, is preparation for compliance

---

[24]Alex Zimmerman, "NYC's Literacy Overhaul Has Earned Wide Support. Now Parents (and Kids) Are Pushing Back," Chalkbeat, April 11, 2024, https://www.chalkbeat.org/newyork/2024/04/10/nyc-schools-literacy-mandate-sees-pushback-hmh-curriculum/.

[25]"Assemblymember Carroll Lauds Governor Hochul's New Science of Reading Proposal," New York State Assembly, January 3, 2024, https://assembly.state.ny.us/mem/Robert-C-Carroll/story/108617.

[26]See Xochitl Gonzalez, "The Schools That Are No Longer Teaching Kids to Read Books," The Atlantic, July 8, 2024, https://www.theatlantic.com/ideas/archive/2024/06/nyc-schools-stopped-teaching-books/678675/.

[27]See, for example, backtracking about "Sold a Story" in Rick Hess, "How a Podcast about Reading Promoted Sweeping Instructional Changes (Opinion)," Education Week, February 18, 2025, https://www.edweek.org/teaching-learning/opinion-how-a-podcast-about-reading-promoted-sweeping-instructional-changes/2025/02.

and servility. There are other American political traditions worth transmitting in schools. The case for liberal education, the proper preparation for life as a self-governing citizen, grounded in books and dedicated, passionate teachers, goes back centuries. Properly conducted, liberal learning is disinterested in ideological outcomes. It emphasizes respect for distinct perspectives, appreciation for art and beauty, skepticism of received wisdom, and capacity for nuanced disagreement. Inasmuch as American curriculum is standardized, it should extend as far as possible opportunities for meaningful reading and writing. Overt book bans are a visible manifestation of a lapsed commitment to promoting open inquiry and empowering teachers to exercise and model liberal habits of mind in public schools.

In 2005, Bill Gates's philanthropy had taken another form. He gave his alma mater, the independent Lakeside School in Seattle, $40 million, and explained, "I want as many students as possible, from as many different backgrounds as possible, to enjoy a Lakeside education." He celebrated an English teacher who "said: 'Bill, you're just coasting. Here are my ten favorite books; read these. Here's my college thesis; you should read it.' She challenged me to do more." He credited her with helping him to "enjoy literature." In Gates's own experience, higher academic standards took the form of a passionate teacher empowered to share the collection of and thoughts about books she had curated for the students she knew personally. In 2014, he told the Washington Post, "I believe in the Common Core because of its substance and what it will do to improve education, and that's the *only* reason I believe in the Common Core. And I have no, you know, this is giving money away. This is philanthropy. This is trying to make sure students have the kind of opportunity I had."[28] Gates had encouragement to value his own mind and to think of reading difficult books as a pleasure. We should, indeed, extend that opportunity further.

---

[28]Layton, "How Bill Gates Pulled Off".

14

A Banned Books Course Syllabus with Historical Notes, Unfortunate Puns, and Books, Lots of Books

Samuel Cohen

English 2000, Studies in English: Banned Books

Prof. Cohen

University of Missouri

Fall 2024

THE COURSE

This is a class about banned books. In particular, this is a class about books that have been banned, challenged, or censored in K-12 schools, in colleges and universities, and in public libraries in the US. We will read, talk, and write about some of these books and about the history of book burning, banning, and censoring in the world and in this country. We will also read, talk, and write about the social and political issues raised, about who gets to decide what we read and teach and lend, and about the value of literary works. Assignments will include reading responses, a critical essay, and a historical context essay. Learning objective: greater awareness of the central issues of book banning, especially in the US and even more especially in Missouri, where you are studying and where most of you were born and raised, a state with a rich history of writers and of people trying to ban their work, a state your instructor is not from but in which he has lived for twenty years and around which he is still trying to get his head.

REQUIRED TEXTS

Alison Bechdel, *Fun Home*

Ray Bradbury, *Fahrenheit 451*

Kate Chopin, *The Awakening*

Dick Gregory, *N******

Toni Morrison, *The Bluest Eye*

Tim O'Brien, *The Things They Carried*

Art Spiegelman, *Maus*

Mark Twain, *Adventures of Huckleberry Finn*

Kurt Vonnegut, *Slaughterhouse-Five*

COURSEWORK

Reading

To get the most out of your experience and participate fully in our discussions, you will need to do the reading for class in advance of the class meeting when it is due, whether it is a novel or secondary reading or both. And remember that reading doesn't mean going through the assigned pages as fast you can, once: it means re-reading, annotating, taking notes in a notebook or on your computer.[1]

Discussion

Discussion will be a big part of the class. We will be talking about important, complicated things because we will be reading important, complicated books, and books like that make you want to talk to other people who are reading them. The fact that people want to keep you from doing that is of course part of the course topic and also a *shanda*.[2]

Daily Reading Responses

At the start of each class, you will write a page in response to the reading for that day. Responses should make clear that you have

---

[1]Also ignore the things that people like that writer in *The Atlantic* say about how college students don't read anymore, especially whole books (Rose Horowitch, "The Elite College Students Who Can't Read Books," *The Atlantic* 334.November 4, 2024, 14–16). Most of you do, even many of you who are only here for the distribution requirement.

[2]A shame, a disgrace. Over the course of the semester, you will also learn some Yiddish.

done the reading; they also offer you the opportunity to reflect, ask questions, or make arguments about what you read. They are also how I take attendance. If you haven't read, your responses will usually show that, and I might make a comment like "I can't actually tell if you read for today, like, at all."[3]

Papers

You will complete two papers of at least four pages each, each with two drafts. The first will be an essay of literary criticism on one of the works we're reading this semester. The second will be an essay on the history of the publication, reception, and banning of one of the works we're reading this semester. The first draft of each assignment will undergo in-class peer review, recorded by the reviewer on a separate sheet of paper. Final drafts will be handed in with first drafts and review comments attached with a paper clip. We will fetishize paper in other ways, including daily reading responses and my incessant badgering to buy copies of the actual books rather than buying them online or renting access to electronic versions, which I understand may be a wee bit cheaper but will rob you of the joy of holding books, marking them up, and watching them soften as you handle them, which helps you to appreciate books in a different way than social media or online shopping catalogues. All writing assignments must be brought to class the day they are due. If you have ChatGPT write your paper for

---

[3] If you have read, and I can read your handwriting, I will marvel at the insightful things you have to say about these books, even and maybe especially the uncomfortable moments in them that make them worth reading and make some people so uncomfortable that they get angry and want to keep them out of your hands.

you, I will know because I will have been reading your in-class writing for weeks and will know you don't know that word.

OFFICE HOURS

Office hours are a time to come ask questions about the material and about your work. You can also come in and surprise me with things you didn't feel comfortable talking about in class, and I say surprise me because sometimes it seems like there is nothing you don't feel comfortable bringing up in class. Which is good! Mostly.

SCHEDULE

Week 1: Introduction, History of Book Banning

On the first day we will introduce ourselves, saying what part of Missouri (or elsewhere) we're from. I will interrupt now and then to ask where the town you say you're from is located in the state, because unless my kids played soccer there there's a good chance I won't know it. We will marvel at the sheer number of towns in the state, notice the clustering of your hometowns around St. Louis and Kansas City but also marking the towns in the bootheel, the Ozarks, the towns near Joplin, pausing to ask if anyone knows that Yakov Smirnoff has a theater there and why.[4] I will be unable to stop myself from noting

---

[4]We will also play the "Oh you're from St. Louis, what high school did you go to?" game and pretend it's not about race and class, just like the difference between being from a city or suburb and from the country isn't also sometimes about these things.

the Missouri towns infamous for recent bans (sorry if you're from Wentzville, I realize it's not your fault). For some reason, you will return to the seat you took the first day for every subsequent class meeting, regardless of the rowless mess the last class leaves every day when they circle up the desks. We will also go through the syllabus.

On the second day I will lecture about the history of book banning, focusing on events from US history but including highlights from elsewhere:

- Qin Shi Huang, first emperor of unified China, who is said to have burned all but one copy of all the books in his kingdom and also to have buried alive hundreds of Confucian scholars, a move only very few of our politicians today would emulate if they could get away with it.

- Ovid, who was exiled from Rome for what he described as "carmen et error," meaning a poem (*Ars Amatoria*, or *The Art of Love*) and a mistake (a personal indiscretion about which we will not speculate); Augustus' action—taken against the author of a seven-year-old poem because Augustus had begun promoting himself as a defender of morality—will represent our first action against literature for ostensible obscenity.

- The legend of Caliph Omar's AD 640 burning of the library at Alexandria, allegedly saying, "If those books are in agreement with the Quran, we have no need of them; and if these are opposed to the Quran, destroy them," a legend promoted by later religious leaders, thus giving us our first example of both religion-motivated banning and the manipulations of the truth so often involved in book bans and contemporaneous and later accounts of them.

- Eight hundred or so years later in Florence, Savonarola[5] organized "bonfires of the vanities" of literature and other things the church deemed sinful (as was he in 1498—burned that is—at the stake, with all his writings), giving us our first example of the many ironies that arise in the history of book banning as well as a chance to note that young people don't know who Tom Wolfe was.[6]

- Not all that long after that and seventy years after Gutenberg printed the first book[7]—a bible—thousands of copies of William Tyndale's English translation of the Bible, the first mass-produced English bible, were also burned, as was he, but not before being strangled.

- Moving to our fair shores, Thomas Morton's 1637 *New English Canaan* was likely the first book banned in what became the US; it was banned because it was a celebration of the culture of the natives and a criticism of their treatment at the hands of the Puritans, written by a man who'd established an offshoot of Plymouth Colony that traded and interacted with the natives—Governor William Bradford saw Morton's people "dancing and frisking together," something not even allowed among themselves, but also trading, and didn't cotton

---

[5]Girolamo Savonarola was a Dominican friar who condemned secularism and championed Christian rule; it is possible that one of you will note parallels to our present moment in our present country.

[6]Wolfe's 1987 novel *Bonfire of the Vanities* was not banned or burned, but it was made into a not very good movie.

[7]Without Gutenberg's movable-type press, historians agree, the Renaissance, Reformation, and modern information age wouldn't have happened; that it was a bible that started it all might be to some one of history's greater ironies, but is certainly a testament to the power of the printed word; the least you can do, then, is bring your books to class.

(Mather)[8] to either, and called Morton's book "an infamous and scurrilous book against many good and chief men of the country, full of lies and slanders and fraught with profane calumnies against their names and persons and the ways of God"; this incident gives us our first domestic example of the intertwining concerns of religion, sex, commerce, and racism.

- In 1650, we had our first book burning, of a pamphlet by William Pynchon called *The Meritorious Price of Our Redemption*, published in England but burned on Boston Common by the Puritan government, which didn't cotton (Mather)[9] to its criticisms of Puritanical Calvinism, giving us a chance to note that most young people don't know who his novelist descendant Thomas is[10]; after a trial that (amazingly) took place in Salem on the same days as our first witch trial, Pynchon avoided having to retract his statements by going back to England.

- Nearly 200 years after Shakespeare's death, in 1807, Thomas Bowdler published a family-friendly version of Shakespeare's works that eliminated words "which cannot with propriety be

---

[8]Cotton Mather was a Puritan clergyman; to "cotton" is to take a liking to; to connect the two is to pun.

[9]I'm so sorry.

[10]I point this out not to shame but to express a wish that reading generally and the reading of novels specifically played a bigger role in American culture now, more like they used to (aware that is a fuddy-duddy lament and also that reading is far from dead); far more important, I point it out so I can have an excuse to quote Thomas Pynchon on puns, which have an unearned reputation as the lowest form of humor while in fact, as Pynchon says in *The Crying of Lot 49* (1966), there is "a high magic to low puns" and so I can again insist on the power and magic of the printed word.

allowed in a family," giving us a name for removing material deemed offensive or improper from a text: "bowdlerizing."[11]

- Back over here again, in 1853, *Uncle Tom's Cabin* was published and became the best-selling novel in the US in the nineteenth century (and second-best book after the Bible), but because of its antislavery stance, it was banned in the Confederacy.[12]

- Weirdly, nobody tried to ban Darwin's *The Origin of Species* in the US until the 1920s—though plenty of people with fond feelings about the biblical creation story were not so fond of Darwin's theory of evolution, it took the theory's entering high school curricula for Tennessee, after the 1925 Scopes ("Monkey") Trial, and other states to ban it, a ban that remained in place in Tennessee until 1967.[13]

- In 1873, US Postal Inspector and creator of the New York Society for the Suppression of Vice[14] Anthony Comstock convinced Congress to pass a law against mailing obscene material, sometimes quite broadly defined, as well as information or drugs related to abortion or contraception, giving us the term "Comstockery" and contemporary

---

[11]What a thing to be remembered for.

[12]There's a possibly apocryphal story that when Lincoln met Harriet Beecher Stowe, he said "So this is the little lady who started this great war," but he didn't note, apocryphally or otherwise, that her sentimentally powerful/powerfully sentimental book also helped make popular negative stereotypes about Black people, including of course the figure of the titular "Uncle Tom."

[13]*Inherit the Wind*, a 1955 play made into a movie in 1960, is the fictionalized story of that trial and is really more about McCarthyism than creationism, giving us an example of a story set in the past being at least as much as about the time of their writing that will be useful later in the semester.

[14]If only they'd made t-shirts!

opponents of abortion a potential tool for outlawing the
mailing of abortifacient mifepristone to states where abortion
is banned.

- An expanded edition of *Leaves of Grass*, Walt Whitman's 1855
collection of poetry, was withdrawn in Boston in 1881 after
the District Attorney threatened criminal prosecution for the
use of explicit language; when this edition of the work was
later published in Philadelphia, it went through five editions
of 1,000 copies each, the first of which sold out in a day,
giving us our first example of an attempted ban leading to an
increase in sales (see "Streisand Effect").[15]

- After the creation of the Irish Free State in 1922, a Committee
on Evil Literature[16] was appointed in 1926, issuing in 1927 the
just as wonderfully named "Report on the Committee on Evil
Literature"; books could be banned if they were considered to
be indecent or obscene, as could newspapers whose content
relied too much on crime as well as works that promoted the
"unnatural" prevention of conception or that advocated for
abortion.

- Speaking of fantastic names, in 1933 the case "U.S. vs. One
Book Called Ulysses" overturned a ban on Joyce's novel
in effect since copies of a 1921 issue of *The Little Review*
containing an excerpt that included masturbation were seized
by the United States Postal Service under the Comstock Act.

---

[15]A term coined to capture the greater exposure that sometimes occurs when people try to
hide information, from singer and actor Barbara Streisand's attempts to suppress a (once)
largely unseen photo of her Malibu home.

[16]Again, where are the t-shirts.

- On May 10, 1933, in most university towns in Germany, nationalist students marched in torchlight parades as part of a self-proclaimed "Action Against the Un-German Spirit," tossing more than 25,000 "un-German" books into bonfires. In all, Nazi Germany burned or otherwise destroyed an estimated 100 million books.

- Back in the US, the McCarthyite Red Scare of the late 1940s and 1950s saw bans of *The Communist Manifesto*, of course, but also of John Steinbeck's 1939 *The Grapes of Wrath* and many other works; McCarthy's career in banning, blacklisting, and otherwise life-ruining ended unhappily, which some might think of as him inheriting the wind (see n.13).

- In 1954, the Comics Code Authority arose in response to parents' concern about the explosion of comics and as a result of Senate hearings, constituting the industry's efforts to police itself in order to avoid government intervention; the drive to censor or even ban comics was aided by Fredric Wertham's 1953 book *Seduction of the Innocent*, scaring the heck out of their parents.

- The 1950s and 1960s also saw ban attempts against Nabokov's *Lolita* (seized by British Customs in 1955), Ginsberg's *Howl* (1957 trial), and Burroughs' *Naked Lunch* (1965 trial), all over obscenity, all attempts eventually rejected in court.

- In 1989, the Ayatollah Khomeini of Iran issued a fatwa ordering Muslims to kill Rushdie following the publication of his novel, *The Satanic Verses*, which the Ayatollah saw as blasphemous, forcing Rushdie into hiding for almost ten years; in 2022, he was stabbed at a reading in upstate New York, sustaining serious injuries and losing sight in one eye, an experience he chronicled in a 2024 memoir, giving us an example both of bravery and of the power of words over attempts to defeat them.

- In 1992, during the war that occurred with the breakup of Yugoslavia, the National and University Library of Bosnia and Herzegovina in Sarajevo was firebombed, destroying more than 1.5 million books, the biggest loss of books in history (additionally, 4,000 rare books, 700 manuscripts, and 100 years of Bosnian newspapers and journals burned).

Next week we'll start reading and discussing books, and we'll get to what's happening in Missouri and nationwide with regard to banned books as we go, which is a lot, all across the state and country: 10,046 instances during the 2023–24 school year of 4,231 unique titles (up from 1,557 in 2022–23), according to PEN America, most astroturfed[17] by national organizations, many by the same people who'd fought against vaccinations and masks during the height of COVID and against CRT, DEI, and LGBTQ and for "school choice," with many of the books chosen being by people and/or about characters from among these minoritized populations;[18] we'll also learn about educational intimidation bills and educational

---

[17]Organized by outside actors rather than local citizens; the opposite of grassroots.
[18]Leading to the inescapable conclusion that bias against same motivates the challenges, regardless of what the challengers claim.

gag orders,[19] and I'll tell you about the magic of the "saving clause," which says the things a bill says plainly it will do (say, criminalize works that contain sexual content and the teachers and librarians who supply them and anybody else involved in the supply chain of those books reaching your hands), it will not actually do, but of course it will.

Once we start reading our books, remember to be ready to write daily reading responses in class and to try to be creative or reflective or at least legible and of course, it's okay to be angry and scared if you are, and you have a right to be.

Weeks 2 & 3: Mark Twain, *Adventures of Huckleberry Finn*

I want us to think about literature in this course in terms of what it can *do* because we too often think about messages—content or themes or issues, what the book "means"—and don't think often enough about how works are made and what it seems like the author is trying to make us experience by making them that way. The Roman poet Horace, in "Ars Poetica" (2,043 years ago, give or take), gave us the idea that literature's purpose is to instruct and delight.[20] What

---

[19]In PEN America's formulation, educational intimidation bills use language about "parental rights" to enable intrusion into curriculum and other decisions; educational gag order bills aim to more directly censor the teaching and, &c. of what are often called "divisive concepts" like race, gender, and sexuality.

[20]Horace says this in a few places in different ways though it never gets its own phrase, unlike *in medias res* or *ab ovo* (other things he said include "even Homer nods" and "purple prose," which nobody knows is from Horace and which you will probably not remember because nobody should expect you to get excited about everything your instructor gets excited about).

does this mean? To instruct—about historical moment or timeless truths?—and to delight—aesthetically, narratively.

For *Huck Finn*, we will talk about aesthetics—Twain's use of dialect and of the forms of the picaresque and the adventure story— and we will talk about instruction—what it's trying to tell us about antebellum social attitudes and human nature. But we will also talk about Louisa May Alcott, author of *Little Women* and of the first attempt to ban this novel, from her perch on the library committee of Concord, MA; about other attempts early and later to get it banned for language, especially its use of the n-word, for its focus on so reprobate a figure as the title character and on the uncomfortable subjects of race and slavery, and for its insufficiently condemning presentation of the flouting of the laws of God and man by Huck like running away, smoking, helping an enslaved man to escape, and becoming real friends with him across the racial divide we still haven't managed to breach. We'll also talk about the ending section when Huck, after the captured Jim has been found and under the influence of Tom Sawyer, assents to keeping Jim prisoner by not immediately freeing him as he and Tom selfishly devise difficult, adventure-story-influenced ways to do so.[21]

We'll also talk briefly about Twain's late, dark work, some of it unpublishable, some held back by him until well after his death; we'll wish we could read Percival Everett's *James* (2024) in class[22];

---

[21]See Hemingway's *Green Hills of Africa* (1935) on this last section of the novel: "That's the real end. The rest is just cheating." Hemingway, Ernest. *Green Hills of Africa*. New York: Scribner, 1935: 21.

[22]But I'll talk in class about its retelling of the story of *Huck Finn* from Jim's point of view excitedly enough to get one of you to read it on your own.

we'll wonder how every single one of you growing up in Missouri wasn't required to read this novel in high school; I'll reflect on the decline in the teaching of novels in high school in favor of test prep and "informational media" or short, nonfictional essays and on the effects of that decline on the preparedness of English majors, on the opting to be or not to be English majors, and on the behavior of the American voter.

Week 4: Kate Chopin, *The Awakening*

This week we'll be reading another Missouri classic, Chopin's feminist novella *The Awakening*.[23] We'll read another hotly debated ending (I've already halfway spoiled *Huck Finn*, so you'll get nothing out of me on this one) and another example of bans purportedly or actually motivated by concerns for propriety and the preservation of society that raise questions about actual motivation and bias and/or about the validity of questioning the rules of that society. We'll talk about why so many of the reviews were hostile, why the St. Louis Mercantile Library felt moved to burn it, how it affected the rest of Chopin's career, and why "Elizabeth Stock's One Story" (from the collection cancelled after/because of the reception of *The Awakening*) is so great (and how the answer is the way it sneakily gives us the intimate, incisive voice of a woman writer whose creative energies are thwarted by societal expectations and judgments). Some of you will hang on to the romance plot of *The Awakening* in spite of the entire book's

---

[23]Chopin is famous for living in and writing about the Louisiana Bayou, but she lived the first twenty and last twenty years of her life in St. Louis.

moving away from that as the happy ending the main character Edna Pontellier is supposed to want; argument will ensue.[24]

Week 5: Ray Bradbury, *Fahrenheit 451*

This week we'll read a book about a country where they've banned books and burn them when they're found, where curiosity is scorned and conformity is king. This will be our "A Little Too on the Nose" week. It will also be a week to reflect on why some books can become canonical without being as respected as other canonical books, something we will return to when we get to Vonnegut.

Week 6: Dick Gregory, *N******

Almost none of you will know who the extraordinary Dick Gregory was, even if you share a hometown in St. Louis, but you will learn about his upbringing in poverty, his standup comedy career, and his Civil Rights Movement activism from this memoir. You will read his thoughts about the use of the n-word by Twain (though Twain never, contrary to what Gregory says in a later memoir[25], calls Jim "N**** Jim" in *Huck Finn*); we'll also talk about his own use of the word for his title (he tells his mother when she hears that word that she'll know

---

[24]Some of you will be intrigued by the story of Chopin's father dying in the Gasconade Bridge collapse, the first major US rail disaster; others will want to hear more about the history of industrialism and racism in the St. Louis of Chopin's childhood, including the 1877 rail strike and the birth of the Veiled Prophet parade; others will want to hear more about the 1904 World's Fair (which Chopin visited, and then died the next day), though few will care about my story of Twain and Henry James having lunch there; others still will want to get back to Edna's desire to free herself. Arguing about what's important in and around books is good. Keeping books from people is bad.

[25]*Callus on My Soul* (2000).

they're talking about his book). We'll talk about attempts to ban the memoir for that very reason and about how there are arguments from more than one side of the political spectrum against using the word.[26]

Weeks 7 & 8: Kurt Vonnegut, *Slaughterhouse-Five*

In Weeks 7 and 8 we'll be reading a novel that (like *Inherit the Wind*) is both about what it's about and about something from another historical moment—in this case, Vonnegut wrote about World War II while thinking about the war the country was in the middle of at the time he wrote it, the war in Vietnam. Vonnegut was not a fan of war and *Slaughterhouse-Five* is not exactly pro-war propaganda itself, making the US look the bad guy for burning Dresden to the ground, and that is one of the reasons this novel has been challenged many times, with famous court cases from Levittown to North Dakota. We'll also talk about the metafictional aspect of the novel—about how Vonnegut puts himself into it, saying of a glimpsed and yet-unnamed character, "That was I. That was me. That was the author of this book," about how he also reflects on the task of writing an anti-war novel, and about how when I introduce metafiction to a class, I can never not say I never met a fiction I didn't like, no matter how loud the groans.[27]

Your first paper, the critical paper, is due at the end of Week 7. In it you will talk about how the book you select instructs and delights, as

---

[26]Again, arguments are good and we should fight for the right to have them, which means fighting for freedom of access to books, the oldest and best place where opinions and arguments and impressions and whole worlds are captured and recorded.
[27]See earlier comments on puns, which are magic.

Horace put it. What does it make us think and feel? Why is it worth keeping on our shelves and in our classrooms?

Week 9: Toni Morrison, *The Bluest Eye*

In addition to your first paper being due, which you will not use AI for because why bother reading books and thinking about books and writing about books at all if you're going to do that, this week we will be reading a novel that's disturbing and upsetting and flawed and brilliant. We will talk about the difference between limiting the exposure of young children to a book and banning it. We will note its presence on the lists of books challenged in Wentzville and St. Louis and elsewhere, and its spot at #3 on the American Library Association's Most Challenged Books of 2024, and we will connect this opposition not just to the prejudices that lead to the banning of books about and by Black people but to the intense discomfort the book itself causes in readers, not that any of the people calling for its banning have actually read it. I will tell you about Mark Smith, then President of Ohio Christian University and member of the Ohio School Board, who said of the novel, "I see an underlying socialist-communist agenda … that is anti what this nation is about."[28] We will also note that Morrison is from Ohio and that the novel is set in Ohio and that she found its banning "ironic at the least." I will share with you that Morrison was an editor for many years at Random House,

---

[28]This will give us an opportunity to reflect on what some people mean when they describe as socialist or communist ideas and practices that are neither, and on whether this is simple ignorance or deliberate demonizing.

bringing to the world important books like *The Black Book* (1974)[29] and *This Bridge Called My Back* (1981), books that explore the harms done to women and Black people in ways that make the Mark Smiths of the world see red (and Red).

Weeks 10 & 11: Art Spiegelman, *Maus*

In Weeks 10 and 11 we will read two books of graphic narrative in which the author tells the story of his mother and father's experience of the Holocaust and of his experience trying to deal with their having lived through the Holocaust. They will all be drawn as mice, while Germans will be cats, Poles pigs, and Americans dogs. There will also be frogs. You will learn about the power simple line drawings and shading can have in Spiegelman's hands, about the complexities of situations that are in some way, like the drawings, seen in black and white. We will also talk about the challenge to *Maus* in Tennessee made ostensibly not because of its depictions of violence but because of a lone panel of a naked woman, the author's mother, who is drawn in a bathtub after committing suicide; Spiegelman said they wanted a "kinder, gentler, fuzzier Holocaust." We will also talk about bans in St. Louis and the rescinded ban of *Maus* in Nixa, Missouri, made under the bill we will have already discussed, to which Spiegelman responded that he would rather the school board "kept their hands off all the books and let students read them."[30] We will also be profoundly sad, and that's not just okay, it's good sometimes.

---

[29] A collection of primary historical documents from which Morrison drew the story that became the germ of her novel *Beloved* (1987).

[30] "Missouri School Board's Decision to Retain Maus is a Positive Move But Removing Six Other Books is Unfortunate, Says PEN America," *PEN America* June 21, 2023.

Weeks 12 & 13: Tim O'Brien, *The Things They Carried*

These weeks will be about Tim O'Brien's novel about the war in Vietnam, another book we're reading this semester that's about war and that attempts to tell what he calls "true war stories," which both can be told and can't really exist, at least not in the way we're used to thinking of them. It's also another book that tries to lay bare the difficulty of telling stories generally, in part through inserting the personal presence of the author through the use of metafiction[31]. I'll have you read Wilfred Owens's poem "Dulce et Decorum Est" (1920) and an example of the jingoistic Great War poetry to which Owen was responding[32] and we'll talk about the conflict between those who want to make war look like fun and those who want to tell the truth about it, and why free access to books about war might be valuable to citizens of countries where they might happen again.[33]

Weeks 14 & 15: Alison Bechdel, *Fun Home*

Our two weeks discussing this graphic novel about homosexuality, the closet, and suicide, all in black and white with occasional blue

---

[31]See, I don't always have to make a pun (this footnote is an example of paralipsis, the rhetorical device of saying a thing by saying you're not saying it, thereby saying it).

[32]I'm looking at you, Jessie Pope's "Who's For the Game" (1915), and yes, it's all there in the title.

[33]Our first day discussing the novel will be November 4; we will studiously avoid discussing the presidential election. On our second day talking about O'Brien, November 6, you will indicate that you'd rather not talk about it but would instead like to distract yourselves by talking about the book. It will become clear that most of you are crushed by the results, though, and we will end a little early with words from me about sleeping, hydrating, and calling home; some of you will indicate that the last bit of advice is not a good one for you.

shading, will be interrupted by Thanksgiving break. I will advise going home and telling your family what you're reading in Banned Books class to see what happens. I will only be half-kidding. Some again will indicate that this would not be a good course of action for you, and I will again be mad at the world for making things so hard for so many of you and for trying to keep you from books that can help you understand your lives.

At the end of the semester, your second paper, on the history of the publication, reception, and banning of one of the books, is due. If you want, you can argue for the value of your book being accessible to students and to anybody who wants to take it out from a library anywhere. It won't be hard, as the history of the way it came to be in the world, the way it's been read, and the way it's been banned—the people behind it and the motivations behind them, both the ostensible ones and the real ones—will make the argument for you.[34]

---

[34]You are of course always welcome to argue for the value of keeping your book from other students or borrowers or even purchasers, as you have been free throughout the semester to make arguments for the sensible restriction of certain books by age minimum or to make arguments for anything you want as long as you do it respectfully. I only ask, at the end of our three or so months together, that you listen to the closing thought of a book we didn't read, Toni Morrison's 1992 novel *Jazz*, which ends with these words from the narrator, revealing itself to be the very book we are reading: "*Say make me, remake me.* You are free to do it and I am free to let you because look, look. Look where your hands are. Now." Look at the book in your hands and let it speak up for itself and for the right of any pair of hands to hold it and any pair of eyes to read it and to then look up and around at the world they're in.

ACKNOWLEDGMENTS

Banning Books in America: Not a How-to is not an instructional manual in book banning, of course, but the essays inside it are how-tos for dedicated, thoughtful writing. Each takes its own angle on the subject of book banning, but they all evince a care for the communities of which they are part and a commitment to telling the truth as they see it in ways that are clear and useful.

So I want to acknowledge and thank everyone who has contributed to this book in spite of being overloaded, as we all are, with our work, with the extra work we've taken on, and with the work of worrying about the world at this intensely worrying time. I also want to thank Haaris Naqvi, Hali Han, and everyone else at Bloomsbury Academic who has helped shepherd this book along. I want to acknowledge the College of Arts & Science and the Office of the Provost of the University of Missouri, who provided me time to write another book that I might have used some of to work on this one. Thank you to the students in my banned books classes, who helped me think harder about the banned books we read and the issues involved in book banning and who renewed my faith in the idea that young people actually do read books, even on their own, in defiance of everyone saying they don't. Thank you finally to my family, who, each in their own way—in their advocacy for the importance of sharing the information that can shape public policy, their thirst for reading and thinking and talking about what they're reading, their writing of papers and poems and songs, and their texting as we begin to spend our lives at geographical removes—remind me that words are important and that nobody should get to keep them from us.

CONTRIBUTORS

Annie Abrams teaches English in New York City. She is the author of *Shortchanged: How Advanced Placement Cheats Students* (Johns Hopkins University Press). Her work has also been published in *Slate, The Chronicle of Higher Education, Liberties, The New Republic, Washington Post*, and elsewhere.

Jacqueline Allain teaches history and social studies at Bard High School Early College-Queens, prior to which she was the coordinator for the Freedom to Learn program at PEN America. She holds a PhD in History from Duke University. Her writing has appeared in the journals *Atlantic Studies, History Compass, Journal of Women's History*, and *Slavery & Abolition*.

Chris Bachelder is the author of several novels, including *U.S.!* and *The Throwback Special*, a finalist for the National Book Award. He teaches at the University of Cincinnati.

Lopamudra Basu is Professor of English at University of Wisconsin-Stout. She is the author of *Ayad Akhtar, the American Nation and its Others After 9/11: Homeland Insecurity* and the co-editor of *Passage to Manhattan: Critical Essays on Meena Alexander*. Her articles have been published in *Humanities, Studies in the Novel, South Asian Review, Women's Studies*, and various anthologies. Her current scholarly interests include trauma studies, post 9/11

American literature, and postcolonial poetry. Her co-edited anthology of poetry, *Sing Slivered Tongue: South Asian Women's Poetry of Trauma in English,* is forthcoming from Yoda Press, New Delhi, in 2025.

Tai Caputo attends Iowa City High School in Iowa City, IA. She is the Executive Editor and Feature Co-Editor of City High's student newspaper, *The Little Hawk.* In 2024, she was the Iowa High School Press Association Writer of the Year. She plans to attend Yale University to pursue academic and musical studies.

Leonard Cassuto is a Professor of English and American Studies at Fordham University and a columnist for *The Chronicle of Higher Education.* He is the author or editor of ten books, none of which has yet been banned, though one—*The Cambridge History of the American Novel*—was described in *The Wall Street Journal* as the work of "barbarians." Cassuto's most recent book is *Academic Writing as if Readers Matter* (Princeton, 2024).

Samuel Cohen teaches English at the University of Missouri. He is author of *After the End of History: American Fiction in the 1990s,* coeditor of *The Legacy of David Foster Wallace* with Lee Konstantinou and *The Clash Takes on the World: Transnational Perspectives on the Only Band That Matters* with James Peacock, series editor of The New American Canon: The Iowa Series in Contemporary Literature and Culture, and author of the textbook *50 Essays: A Portable Anthology.* He is working on a book on the history of university presses in the US, *Higher Learning by the Book.*

Emily Drabinski is Associate Professor and Chair of the Queens College Graduate School of Library and Information Studies at the City University of New York. She was president of the American Library Association from July 2023 to July 2024.

Brian K. Goodman is Assistant Professor in the Department of English at Arizona State University, where he is also a faculty affiliate of the Melikian Center for Russian, Eurasian & East European Studies and the Center for Jewish Studies. His first book, *The Nonconformists: American and Czech Writers across the Iron Curtain* (Harvard UP, 2023), received the Pamela Jensen Award from the American Political Science Association. His writing on issues related to censorship, dissent, and free expression has appeared in *Public Books* and the *Los Angeles Review of Books*.

Emily Harris serves on the board of Annie's Foundation, a grassroots organization fighting censorship in Iowa schools. When book bans targeted her daughter's classroom, she joined five other moms to push back—exposing the growing influence of extremist groups at the local level. Emily has filed public records requests that uncovered hundreds of banned books, written advocacy materials used across the state, and helped distribute more than 12,500 banned books to students and families. She is also a full-time intellectual property attorney, holding a biology degree from Grinnell College and a J.D. from the University of Iowa College of Law.

Lydia Millet's newest book is *Atavists: Stories* (2025). She has written eighteen novels and story collections and a nonfiction work, *We Loved It All: A Memory of Life* (2024). Her novel *A Children's Bible* (2020) was a finalist for the National Book Award in fiction and a *New York*

Times Book Review's Best 10 Books of 2020. Millet has won fiction awards from the American Academy of Arts and Letters and PEN-Center USA and has been a finalist for the Pulitzer Prize; since 1999 she has also worked as a writer and editor at the Center for Biological Diversity.

Aaron Santesso is Professor of Literature at Georgia Tech. He has authored and edited several books, including *A Careful Longing: The Poetics and Problems of Nostalgia*; his articles have appeared in *ELH*, *Modern Philology*, *Modern Fiction Studies*, and elsewhere. With David Rosen (Trinity College), he is author of *The Watchman in Pieces: Surveillance, Literature, and Liberal Personhood* (Yale University Press, 2013), which received the MLA's James Russell Lowell Prize for outstanding book of the year. His work with Rosen as also been published in *Slate*, *The Chronicle of Higher Education*, *American Literary History*, *ELH*, *Law and Literature*, and elsewhere.

Amardeep Singh is Professor of English at Lehigh University. He is the author of two scholarly books, and has been involved in a number of digital humanities projects, including "African American Poetry: A Digital Anthology" and "Toni Morrison: A Teaching and Learning Resource Collection." His essay on the theme of names in Morrison, "Catachresis at the Origin: Names and Power in Toni Morrison's Fiction," appeared in *South Central Review* in 2024. His next book project is called *The Archive Gap: Race and Representation in the Digital Humanities*.

Carol Weston is the author of sixteen books including *Girltalk: All the Stuff Your Sister Never Told You* and *Speed of Life*. She's been Dear Carol of *Girls' Life Magazine* since its first issue. Carol majored in French and Spanish Comparative Literature at Yale, graduating *summa cum laude*. She has taught writing at Middlebury College and The New York Society Library.

Jeremy C. Young is the senior advisor for strategic initiatives at the American Association of Colleges and Universities (AAC&U). His past roles include the director of state and higher education policy at PEN America, as well as assistant professor of history and director of the Institute of Politics and Public Affairs at Utah Tech University. He holds a BA in history and music from St. Mary's College of Maryland and an MA and PhD in US history from Indiana University, and is the author of *The Age of Charisma: Leaders, Followers, and Emotions in American Society, 1870–1940* (Cambridge, 2017).

BIBLIOGRAPHY

American Association of University Professors, "1940 Statement of Principles on Academic Freedom and Tenure" (American Association of University Professors, 1940), https://www.aaup.org/report/1940-statement-principles-academic-freedom-and-tenure.

American Library Association. "Top 10 Most Challenged Books of 2024." https://www.ala.org/bbooks/frequentlychallengedbooks/top10.

Appiah, Kwame Anthony. "Can I Ban Books from my Front-Yard Little Free Library?" *The New York Times* 19 January 2025, 14–15. https://www.nytimes.com/2025/01/10/magazine/little-free-library-ethics.html.

"Assemblymember Carroll Lauds Governor Hochul's New Science of Reading Proposal," New York State Assembly, January 3, 2024, https://assembly.state.ny.us/mem/Robert-C-Carroll/story/108617.

Associated Press. "Missouri District Rescinds Decision to Ban Toni Morrison Book." February 27, 2022. Accessed via NBC News here: https://www.nbcnews.com/news/nbcblk/missouri-district-rescinds-decision-ban-toni-morrison-book-rcna17858.

Baijnath, Narend et al., "Magna Charta Universitatum 2020" (Magna Charta Observatory, March 12, 2020), https://www.magna-charta.org/magna-charta-universitatum/mcu2020.

Barnes, Brooks. "Snow White and the Seven Kajillion Controversies." *The New York Times*, 27 March 2025. https://www.nytimes.com/2025/03/20/business/snow-white-movie-controversies.html.

Bazyler, Michael J. "Holocaust Denial Laws and Other Legislation Criminalizing Promotion of Nazism." *Yad Vashem* https://www.yadvashem.org/holocaust/holocaust-antisemitism/holocaust-denial-laws.html.

Benedict, Glen J. "It is Not Just the Quantity: Book Challenges in 2021 and Beyond," in Shannon M. Oltmann (ed), *The Fight Against Book Bans: Perspectives from the Field*, 11–21. New York: Bloomsbury. 2023.

Board of the Chippewa Valley Civil Liberties Union. Letter to Superintendent Zydowsky 12 May 2017. https://www.aclu-wi.org/en/news/chippewa-valley-aclu-chapter-stands-educational-freedom-controversy-over-book.

"Books belong in school; attend read-in Thur." Community Voices for Public Education, accessed February 25, 2025, https://www.houstoncvpe.org/books_belong_in_school_attend_read_in_thur.

Burt, Richard. "Introduction: The 'New' Censorship," in Burt, Richard, ed., *The Administration of the Aesthetic: Censorship, Political Criticism and the Public Sphere*, ed. Richard Burt. Minneapolis: Minnesota University Press, 1994.

Cain, Timothy Reese. "Accreditation, Academic Freedom, and Institutional Autonomy: Historical Precedents and Modern Imperatives," *AAUP Journal of Academic Freedom* 14 (2023): 12.

Chuh, Kandice. "Too Sad, Too Diverse, Too Poetic." *PMLA*, 138.1 (2023): 218–22.

Coleman, David and Susan Pimentel. "The Role of Fiction in the High School English Language Arts Classroom," *The Huffington Post*, December 11, 2012, https://www.huffpost.com/entry/the-role-of-fiction-in-th_b_2279782.

Collins, Jason. Personal Interview, Menomonie WI, 22 January 2025. *CommonLit*. https://www.commonlit.org/en (Accessed 25 February 2025).

Conroy, Pat. "Anatomy of a Divorce." *Atlanta Magazine*, 1 November 1978. https://www.atlantamagazine.com/great-reads/anatomy-of-a-divorce/.

Copestake, Ian D. "Allen Ginsberg," in *Censorship: A World Encyclopedia*. Routledge, 2001.

D'Amico Pawlewicz, Diana. *Blaming Teachers: Professionalization Policies and the Failure of Reform in American History*. Rutgers University Press, 2020.

Darnton, Robert. *Censors at Work: How States Shaped Literature*. Norton, 2014.

Doniger, Wendy. *The Hindus: An Alternative History*. Penguin. 2009.

Elkind, Peter. "How Business Got Schooled in the War Over Common Core," *Fortune Magazine*, December 23, 2015, https://fortune.com/longform/common-core-standards/.

Fair Work Commission (Australia). "A Guide to Interest-Based Bargaining," 12 August 2024. https://www.fwc.gov.au/documents/resources/guide-interest-based-bargaining.pdf.

"First Mein Kampf reprint in Germany since war set for sixth print run." *The Guardian*, 7 January 2017. https://www.theguardian.com/world/2017/jan/03/first-mein-kampf-reprint-germany-since-war-sixth-print-run-hitler.

Friedman, Jonathan and James Tager, "Educational Gag Orders: Legislative Restrictions on the Freedom to Read, Learn, and Teach" (PEN America, November 8, 2021), https://pen.org/report/educational-gag-orders/.

Gallagher, Kelly. *Readicide*. Routledge, 2009.

Gates, Bill. "Prepared Remarks, National Conference of State Legislatures (NCSL)." Gates Foundation, July 20, 2009. https://www.gatesfoundation.org/Ideas/Speeches/2009/07/bill-gates-national-conference-of-state-legislatures-ncsl.

Gessen, Masha. "In the Shadow of the Holocaust." *The New Yorker*, 9 December 2023. https://www.newyorker.com/news/the-weekend-essay/in-the-shadow-of-the-holocaust.

Ginsberg, Allen. *Howl and Other Poems*. City Lights, 1956.

Ginsberg, Allen. "Kral Majales," in *Planet News, 1961–1967*. City Lights Books, 1968.

Glatman, Joshua. "Author Julie Otsuka Headlines the Humanities Symposium Keynote Address," University Wire, 4 April 2023. https://thegreyhound. org/13727/news/author-julie-otsuka-headlines-the-humanities-symposium-keynote-address/.

Goodman, Brian K. *The Nonconformists: American and Czech Writers across the Iron Curtain* (Cambridge: Harvard UP, 2023).

Gonzalez, Xochitl. "The Schools That Are No Longer Teaching Kids to Read Books," *The Atlantic*, July 8, 2024, https://www.theatlantic.com/ideas/archive/2024/06/nyc-schools-stopped-teaching-books/678675/.

Greene, Peter. "Common Core Testing and the Fracturing of Literature," Forbes, December 4, 2018, https://www.forbes.com/sites/petergreene/2018/11/09/common-core-testing-and-the-fracturing-of-literature/.

Hájek, Igor. "Americká bohéma," *Světová literatura* 4, no. 6 (1959): 207–33.

Harris, Elizabeth A. and Alexandra Alter. "With Rising Book Bans, Librarians Have Come Under Attack." *The New York Times*, 6 July 2022. https://www.nytimes.com/2022/07/06/books/book-ban-librarians.html.

Harris, Maya Shimizu. "Wyoming Lawmakers Set for Showdown over UW Gender Studies, Diversity Office," *WyoFile*, February 21, 2024, https://wyofile.com/wyoming-lawmakers-set-for-showdown-over-uw-gender-studies-diversity-office/.

Hawkins, Stacy. "Sometimes Diversity Trumps Academic Freedom." *The Chronicle of Higher Education* 28 February 2023. https://www.chronicle.com/article/sometimes-diversity-trumps-academic-freedom.

Hemingway, Ernest. *Green Hills of Africa*. Scribner, 1935.

Herald Reports, "Complaint Filed by Local Moms For Liberty Chapter Rejected by State," *Williamson Herald*, November 30, 2021, https://www.williamsonherald.com/features/education/complaint-filed-by-local-moms-for-liberty-chapter-rejected-by-state/article_81146dc4-518f-11ec-9d9a-237001a4ab9f.html.

Hess, Rick. "How a Podcast about Reading Promoted Sweeping Instructional Changes (Opinion)," *Education Week*, February 18, 2025, https://www.edweek.org/teaching-learning/opinion-how-a-podcast-about-reading-promoted-sweeping-instructional-changes/2025/02.

Horwitch, Rose. "The Elite College Students Who Can't Read Books," *The Atlantic*, October 1, 2024, https://www.theatlantic.com/magazine/archive/2024/11/the-elite-college-students-who-cant-read-books/679945/.

Houston, Jeanne Wakatsuki, and James D Houston. *Farewell to Manzanar: A True Story of Japanese American Experience During and After the World War II Internment*. Houghton Mifflin, 1973.

Johnson, Nadine Farid. "The US Is Inspiring Education Censorship Elsewhere,"
    Aljazeera, January 4, 2023, https://www.aljazeera.com/opinions/2023/1/4/
    the-us-is-exporting-education-censorship-2.

Layton, Lynsey. "How Bill Gates Pulled off the Swift Common Core Revolution,"
    The Washington Post, June 7, 2014, http://www.washingtonpost.com/politics/
    how-bill-gates-pulled-off-the-swift-common-core-revolution/2014/06/07/
    a830e32e-ec34-11e3-9f5c-9075d5508f0a_story.html.

Lehrer-Small, Asher. "ARE HISD Students Checking out Fewer Books at Schools
    without Librarians? It's Hard to Say.," *Houston Landing*, February 20, 2024,
    https://houstonlanding.org/hisd-librarian-book-checkout-mike-miles-
    school-overhaul-nes/.

Lelyveld, Joseph. *Great Soul: Mahatma Gandhi and his Struggle with India.*
    Vintage, 2012.

"Library killer or book lover?" *Houston Chronicle*, accessed February 25, 2025,
    https://www.houstonchronicle.com/opinion/editorials/article/miles-hisd-
    houston-libraries-books-18340935.php.

Linane, Rory (2022). "Wisconsinites Rally Around Book Rejected by
    Muskego Board for Focus on Japanese Experience." *Milwaukee Journal
    Sentinel*, 18 July. Available online: https://eu.jsonline.com/story/news/
    education/2022/07/18/rally-backs-book-rejected-muskego-focus-japanese-
    americans/10051434002/.

Lishaugen, Roar and Šmejkalová, "Reading East of the Berlin Wall," *PMLA* 134,
    no. 1 (January 2019): 178–87.

Little, Anita. "On the Frontlines of the Fight Against Classroom Censorship."
    ACLU Website, September 15, 2023. https://www.aclu.org/news/free-speech/
    teachers-frontlines-classroom-censorship.

Lueders, Bill. "Wisconsin School District Rejects Book About Japanese
    Internment." *Wisconsin Examiner*, 22 June 2022. https://wisconsinexaminer.
    com/2022/06/22/wisconsin-school-district-rejects-book-about-japanese-
    internment.

Mayer v. Monroe County Community School …, accessed February 25, 2025
    https://caselaw.findlaw.com/court/us-7th-circuit/1233551.html.

Mehta, Deepa, dir. *Fire.* New Delhi: Kaleidoscope Entertainment and Trial by
    Fire, 1996.

Mehta, Deepa, dir. Water. Toronto: David Hamilton Productions, 2005.

Marin, Emily. "'DEI Must Die': Nebraska Bill Would Ban University Diversity
    Pledges," *The College Fix*, March 8, 2024, https://www.thecollegefix.com/dei-
    must-die-nebraska-bill-would-ban-university-diversity-pledges/.

Markham, Madison and Tessalyn Magnusson (2024). "The State of Book Bans:
    Wisconsin's Battle with Parental Rights," 18 July 2024. Available online: https://
    pen.org/the-state-of-book-bans-wisconsins-battle-with-parental-rights/.

Meehan, Kasey Meehan et al., "Banned in the USA: Beyond the Shelves," Banned in the USA (PEN America, November 1, 2024), https://pen.org/report/beyond-the-shelves/.

Mellinkoff, Abe. "Morning Report: Iron Curtain on the Embarcadero," *San Francisco Chronicle*, March 28, 1957.

"Missouri School Board's Decision to Retain Maus is a Positive Move But Removing Six Other Books is Unfortunate, Says PEN America," *PEN America* 21 Jun. 2023.

Mistry, Rohinton. *Such a Long Journey*, Knopf, 1991.

Morgan, Bill. *Howl on Trial: The Battle for Free Expression*. City Lights Books, 2006.

Morrison, Toni. "Nobel Prize Lecture." December 7, 1993. https://www.nobelprize.org/prizes/literature/1993/morrison/lecture/.

Morrison, Toni. "Introduction" to *The Oxford Mark Twain: Adventures of Huckleberry Finn*, edited by Shelley Fisher Fishkin. Oxford University Press, 1996.

Morrison, Toni. "Peril." In Toni Morrison, Ed. *Burn This Book: PEN Writers Speak Out On the Power of the Word*. New York: Harper, 2009.

Oltmann, Shannon. M. "Libraries in the 2020s" in Shannon M. Oltmann (ed), *The Fight Against Book Bans: Perspectives from the Field*, 1–7. Bloomsbury, 2023.

Otsuka, Julie. *When the Emperor was Divine*. Anchor, 2007.

Page, Benedicte. "New Huckleberry Finn edition censors 'n-word.'" *The Guardian*, January 5, 2011. https://www.theguardian.com/books/2011/jan/05/huckleberry-finn-edition-censors-n-word.

PEN America, "PEN America Index of Educational Gag Orders," Spreadsheet, n.d. https://airtable.com/appg59iDuPhlLPPFp/shrtwubfBUo2tuHyO/tblZ40w5HLBuTK9vs/viw5lFPxKHGkamF0k?blocks=hide.

PEN America, "PEN America Index of School Book Bans – 2023-2024," Table, 2024 2023, https://pen.org/book-bans/pen-america-index-of-school-book-bans-2023-2024/.

Pinski, Hannah. "'We Aren't Always for Diversity.' Kentucky Senate Advances Limits on DEI Programs," *Louisville Courier Journal*, February 13, 2024, https://www.courier-journal.com/story/news/politics/2024/02/13/senate-bill-6-limiting-diversity-programs-at-kentucky-colleges-advances/72589142007/.

Pondiscio, Robert. "A Missed Opportunity for Common Core," *Education Next*, March 26, 2020, https://www.educationnext.org/missed-opportunity-common-core/.

Powers, Pamela. "Menomonie School District to Review the Role of Religion in Curriculum." *Leader Telegram*, 25 April 2017. https://www.leadertelegram.

com/news/front-page/menomonie-school-district-to-review-role-of-religion-in-curriculum/article_a3a53943-ca80-5655-8c2d-15973de7a54d.html.

Ramesh, Sruthi. "WSD Bans Book, Deeming the Selection Inappropriate" *LHS Today*, January 31, 2022. https://lhstoday.org/31945/news/wsd-bans-book-deeming-the-selection-inappropriate/.

Raval, Sheela, and Madhu Jain. "Deepa Mehta's Film Fire Creates a Furore." *India Today*, 21 December 1998. https://www.indiatoday.in/magazine/society-the-arts/films/story/19981221-controversial-film-fire-is-sent-back-to-censor-board-matter-taken-to-court-827561-1998-12-20.

Ravitch, Diane. "Why I Oppose Common Core Standards," *The Washington Post*, February 26, 2013, https://www.washingtonpost.com/news/answer-sheet/wp/2013/02/26/why-i-oppose-common-core-standards-ravitch/.

Rufo, Christopher F. "D.E.I. Programs Are Getting in the Way of Liberal Education," *New York Times*, July 27, 2023, https://www.nytimes.com/2023/07/27/opinion/christopher-rufo-diversity-desantis-florida-university.html.

Rushdie, Salman (1988), *The Satanic Verses*. London: Viking.

Rushdie, Salman (1995), The *Moor's Last Sigh*. London: J. Cape.

Schoolyard News, "Thirty-One Mission Hill School Faculty Protest Wit and Wisdom Curriculum," Medium, July 14, 2020, https://schoolyardnews.com/thirty-one-mission-hill-school-faculty-protest-wit-and-wisdom-curriculum-2e3b3abc4f8a.

Schrecker, Ellen. "Yes, These Bills Are the New McCarthyism." *Academe Blog* 12 September 2021, https://academeblog.org/2021/09/12/yes-these-bills-are-the-new-mccarthyism/.

Schwab, Tim. *The Bill Gates Problem : Reckoning with the Myth of the Good Billionaire*. First edition. New York: Metropolitan Books, Henry Holt and Company, 2023.

Šmejkalová, Jiřina. "Censoring Canons: Transitions and Prospects of Literary Institutions in Czechoslovakia," in *The Administration of the Aesthetic: Censorship, Political Criticism and the Public Sphere*, ed. Richard Burt. Minnesota University Press, 1994.

"Speech by Federal Chancellor Angela Merkel before the Knesset, 18 March 2008 in Jerusalem." https://www.bundesregierung.de/breg-de/service/bulletin/rede-von-bundeskanzlerin-dr-angela-merkel-796170.

Tampio, Nicholas. *Common Core: National Education Standards and the Threat to Democracy* Johns Hopkins University Press, 2018.

Thapar, Romila (2023), Our *History, Their History, Whose History*. Calcutta: Seagull.

Uhlir, Joyce. "Menomonie Matters." https://menomoniematters.substack.com/p/love-makes-a-family.

"University Autonomy in Europe IV: The Scorecard 2023" (European University Association, March 7, 2023), https://www.eua.eu/publications/reports/university-autonomy-in-europe-iv-the-scorecard-2023.html.

Walker, Mark E. Pernell v. Florida Board of Governors of the State University System (United States District Court Northern District of Florida Tallahassee Division November 17, 2022).

Waxman, Olivia B. "Why Toni Morrison's Books Are So Often the Target of Book Bans." *Time*, January 31, 2022. https://time.com/6143127/toni-morrison-book-bans/.

"What Students Read," *Los Angeles Times*, December 27, 2012, https://www.latimes.com/opinion/editorials/la-xpm-2012-dec-27-la-ed-1227-fiction-20121227-story.html.

Winstead, Chantal. "The 'Beloved' Bill: The Controversy of HB 516." April 24, 2016. *National Council of Teachers of English*. https://ncte.org/report/the-beloved-bill-the-controversy-of-hb-516/.

Wögerbauer, Michael, Petr Píša, Petr Šámal, Pavel Janáček, et. al., editors. *In the Public Interest Censorship and the Social Regulation of Literature in Modern Czech Culture, 1749–2014*. Academia, 2015.

Woodruff, Betsy. "Goodbye Liberal Arts?" *The National Review*, December 13, 2012, https://www.nationalreview.com/2012/12/goodbye-liberal-arts-betsy-woodruff/.

Yarrow, Andrew L. "Allen Ginsberg's 'Howl' in a New Controversy," *New York Times*, January 6, 1968. https://www.nytimes.com/1988/01/06/arts/allen-ginsberg-s-howl-in-a-new-controversy.html.

Young, Jeremy C. "Christopher Rufo's Alarming and Deceptive Crusade Against Public Universities," *TIME*, August 30, 2023, https://time.com/6309612/christopher-rufo-public-universities-deceptive-essay/.

Young, Jeremy C. "PEN America Endorses the Magna Charta Universitatum 2020," pen.org, October 9, 2024, https://pen.org/pen-america-endorses-the-magna-charta-universitatum-2020/.

Young, Jeremy C., Jonathan Friedman, and Kasey Meehan. "America's Censored Classrooms 2023: Lawmakers Shift Strategies as Resistance Rises," America's Censored Classrooms (PEN America, November 9, 2023), https://pen.org/report/americas-censored-classrooms-2023/.

Youngkin, Glenn. Campaign ad, October 25, 2021. Accessed on X here: https://x.com/GlennYoungkin/status/1452668527358402582.

Yousafzai, Malala, Christina Lamb, and Go Big Read. *I Am Malala: The Girl Who Stood up for Education and Was Shot by the Taliban*, Little, Brown, & Company, 2013.

Zimmerman, Alex. "NYC's Literacy Overhaul Has Earned Wide Support. Now
Parents (and Kids) Are Pushing Back." *Chalkbeat*, April 11, 2024, https://
www.chalkbeat.org/newyork/2024/04/10/nyc-schools-literacy-mandate-
sees-pushback-hmh-curriculum/.
Zimmerman, Jonathan. *Whose America?: Culture Wars in the Public Schools.*
University of Chicago Press, 2022.

INDEX